WITHDRAWN

THE TREMBLING EARTH

OTHER BOOKS BY FREDERIC GOLDEN

The Moving Continents
Quasars, Pulsars, and Black Holes
Colonies in Space

THE TREMBLING EARTH

probing & predicting quakes

frederic golden

charles scribner's sons   new york

Grateful acknowledgment is made to the following for illustrations used in this book:

U.S. Geological Survey (frontispiece, pages 9, 10, 11, 27, 43, 56, 76); Bruce A. Bolt (19); Science Museum, London (38; photo copyright by Science Museum); California Institute of Technology (47, 155); Columbia University (110, 143)

Copyright © 1983 Frederic Golden

Library of Congress Cataloging in Publication Data
Golden, Frederic.   The trembling earth.
Bibliography: p.
Includes index.
1. Seismology.   2. Earthquake prediction.
I. Title.
QE534.2G64   1983   551.2′2   83-3262
ISBN 0-684-17884-2

This book published simultaneously in the
United States of America and in Canada —
Copyright under the Berne Convention.

All rights reserved. No part of this book
may be reproduced in any form without the
permission of Charles Scribner's Sons.

1 3 5 7 9 11 13 15 17 19   F/C   20 18 16 14 12 10 8 6 4 2

Printed in the United States of America.

To Nancy,
who tolerated the tremors
with extraordinary grace

CONTENTS

Introduction   ix
1 The Day That San Francisco Died   1
2 Oxen, Catfish, and Angry Gods   18
3 Rumbles in the Heartland   36
4 An Earthquake Primer   53
5 Continents on the Move   75
6 Probing the Planet   96
7 The Visionaries Prevail   117
8 Seismologists Who Are Seers   136
Selected Bibliography   167
Index   169

INTRODUCTION

When the first astronauts traveled into space, they saw the earth as it had never been seen before: as a solitary sphere, framed by the starry night, with deep blue seas, shimmering white clouds, and rich green vegetation. By contrast, the moon and, indeed, all the other members of the sun's family looked bleak and lifeless.

The view from space had a profoundly moving effect, not only on the astronauts, but on much of humanity as well. It created an awareness of the planet's fragile beauty and uniqueness, stirred a new global consciousness, and helped encourage the beginnings of the environmental movement. As Adlai Stevenson, the American ambassador to the United Nations, said in those early days of space exploration: "We all travel together, passengers on a little spaceship, dependent on its vulnerable supplies of air and soil; all committed for our safety to its security and peace, preserved from annihilation only by the care, the work, and the love we give our fragile craft."

Stevenson's fragile craft sustains life because it is at just the right distance from the sun to permit the existence of liquid water. If the earth were any closer to the solar fires, the life-sustaining fluid would boil away; any farther away, the precious water would freeze. The earth's surface is also shielded by a protective atmosphere that blocks out deadly solar radiation that would wipe out all but the most durable creatures. Not only is the earth a sanctuary for life, it is also a forgiving place. It has been able to withstand some of the worst ravages visited upon it. Polluted rivers and streams cleanse themselves. Forests and fields eventually recover from neglect or abuse. Given enough time, natural processes will even heal such human-inflicted scars as hills torn up by strip mines and holes carved out of the earth by explosions.

But the earth can also be very cruel. Just as it encourages life to flourish, it can destroy it. At its disposal are any number of weapons, including fires, floods, and violent storms. There are also biological time bombs like the outbreak of epidemics or such long-term climatological hazards as drought or the onset of a new ice age. These calamities are forceful reminders that nature can be harsh and unforgiving.

At no time is this aspect of the earth more apparent than during an earthquake. When the earth unleashes its full might in an area that is densely inhabited, the devastation can be complete. There is hardly an event in nature capable of doing so much damage in so short a period of time. As the earth's population increases, and people become more tightly packed together, the danger to life will increase.

Usually striking without warning, capable of crumbling almost anything in their path when they shake the ground with maximum force, earthquakes are an example of nature at its fiercest. They have been a peril for as long as humans have walked the planet. And, of course, even the dinosaurs felt the earth move under them. In ancient times, people interpreted earthquakes as an act of heavenly displeasure. For those who

Introduction

lived in quake-prone regions, the only recourse was to adhere to strict rules of moral conduct that could perhaps appease the gods and contain their anger. A sacrifice or two might provide added protection.

The formula has obviously not worked very well. Since the beginnings of history 10,000 years ago, perhaps as many as 75 million people have been killed directly or indirectly by earthquakes. The toll makes quakes one of the earth's great destroyers of life, exceeded only by even more remorseless killers such as war and disease. And the danger continues. Even in this scientific age, when humans can coax energy from the nucleus of the atom, send travelers to far-off worlds, and retool the basic genetic structures of life itself, quakes still flaunt their power. Each year thousands of people perish when the earth goes on its rampages.

Now this killer may finally be brought to account. The hope arises not from the fraudulent claims of the self-styled prognosticators who have been boasting of their special ability to forecast and sometimes even to stop quakes down through the ages. Rather it stems from the remarkable recent advances of earth scientists in getting at the secrets of the earth's interior. Using this information, they are coming ever closer to the day when they will be able to foretell with almost clockwork regularity when, where, and with what force an earthquake will strike. Already, many successful predictions have been made, although there have also been some major failures.

The acquisition of this new skill, even if it is still an imperfect one, is an extraordinary achievement. It is the end product of work by numerous scientists, some of them well known, others only footnotes in the history of seismology—the special discipline dealing with the study of the earth's shaking. This book discusses, through the lives of some of the people who played major roles in this great intellectual triumph, how it came about; how it affects our understanding of the earth and its quakes; and what the progress in the earth sciences, in particular seismology, holds for the future.

Much of the emphasis is on disaster: mighty forces creating incredible destruction and horrifying human losses. Fortunately, only a handful of the up to 800,000 quakes that occur in a typical year are powerful enough to take any lives. Most quakes are beyond human perception, barely moving the needles of the sensitive instruments that have been designed to record them. The majority jar the ocean bottom, far from any place where they can do harm. And this accounting does not include the vastly greater number of tiny micro tremors that constantly seem to be vibrating our world. No doubt about it, we live on a trembling earth.

In fact, there are even some good things to be said about quakes. Aside from the mental challenges they have provided for those trying to fathom their mysteries, they have helped shape some of the most spectacular scenery on the face of spaceship earth: the ruggedly beautiful coastline of California, the jagged peaks of the Alps, the breathtaking valleys nestled between towering mountains, to mention only a few examples. These are, as Don Anderson, director of the seismological laboratory at the California Institute of Technology, points out, all products of an ongoing geological process that is forming and re-forming the earth.

The story of this eternal process is told here in nontechnical terms, as simply and as colorfully as possible without doing injustice to the underlying concepts. The book is also highly selective, stressing those events and scientists that seem especially revelant while omitting others that have been described in detail in many other places. Some topics, although obviously important, have been mentioned only in passing, such as the effort to find new building techniques for putting up quake-resistant structures.

No effort has been made to write a definitive treatise on seismology, not that this lay author would presume to attempt such an undertaking. Nonetheless, in writing this book and in covering the advances in the earth sciences for *Time* magazine, the author has relied on the help and counsel of many distinguished seismologists, including Don Anderson, C. Barry Raleigh, Christopher Scholz, and Lynn R. Sykes. In addition, D.W. Caldwell of Boston University made valuable suggestions on the manuscript itself. To them go grateful thanks and absolution from any sins in the text. If the writing has been guided by any single goal, it is the hope that some readers may be sufficiently inspired by the achievements described herein to look further into the expanding world of the earth sciences.

THE TREMBLING EARTH

A young survivor surveys the wreckage of downtown San Francisco after the city's devastating 1906 earthquake.

1 THE day THAT SAN francisco died

SAN FRANCISCO, October 19. . . .

It is late Friday afternoon on a balmy autumn day in San Francisco. Throngs of tourists are mingling with local young people in Ghiradelli Square, the reconstructed showcase area overlooking the waterfront. The visitors wander in and out of restored old brick factory buildings, browse in the many shops, buy snacks and souvenirs from sidewalk vendors, and snap away with their cameras.

Clanging up and down Powell and Hyde Streets, the city's venerable cable cars are as crowded as always, with the inevitable daredevils clinging to their sides. At Lefty O'Doul's pub, off Union Square, patrons have begun to arrive for an early-evening drink under walls bedecked with photographs of athletes, politicians, and other notables. In Chinatown's restaurants, white-garbed chefs sing out their orders in Cantonese as they prepare for the dinner hour.

The nightly exodus has begun. In the downtown business district, thousands of workers are pouring out of offices and shops, eager to get to their homes in the suburbs across San Francisco Bay or down the peninsula. BART, the Bay Area Rapid Transit

System, is jammed. Passengers in the subway cars seem as closely packed as the shellfish on display at Fisherman's Wharf. The decks are also full on the ferry to Sausalito, the arty peninsular colony across the bay. On the freeways and at the approaches to the Golden Gate and Bay Bridges, cars are inching along bumper-to-bumper. But spirits are uniformly high. Everyone is looking forward to the weekend.

It is exactly 4:35 P.M., according to the hands on a big clock outside a department store. They will not move any farther.

With no forewarning, this ordinary rush-hour scene quickly becomes a nightmare. The ground starts shaking and swaying with incredible violence. A deafening rumble, louder than the roar of 100 freight trains, splits the air. People in the streets cry out in panic as sidewalks and roadways crack and tons of glass, stone, and masonry come tumbling down from buildings. High above the city, a pianist entertaining patrons in the Top of the Mark, the famed rooftop cocktail lounge, is stopped abruptly while playing "I Left My Heart in San Francisco."

Some older structures collapse immediately, like a youngster's fragile house of cards. Others totter alarmingly. Pedestrians and cars are crushed in the downpour of debris falling off buildings. The toll is especially high along Chinatown's Grant Street, which bristles with brightly colored signs, Oriental carvings, and other vulnerable ornamentation. This usually festive street is transformed into a thoroughfare of death.

No one really needs to be told what is happening. In a few horrifying seconds, the Bay Area's millions realize that the long dormant faults in the earth beneath them have suddenly and ferociously reawakened. The great earthquake, forecast so often by scientists and psychics alike, is finally devastating San Francisco. As the ground's vibrations increase, glass-and-steel office towers and fashionable high-rise buildings rock crazily back and forth like ships in a storm-tossed sea. Those people caught inside stagger about, unable to keep their balance, while books, plants, and pictures are crashing all about them in a blizzard of flying objects. Windows shatter and walls crack. The buildings shake so violently that furniture, office equipment, and even people are shot out of the upper floors.

As power lines snap, lights blink out across the city. Radios and television sets fall silent. Elevators jar to a halt, trapping hundreds of office workers inside them. Fires seem to erupt everywhere, ignited by short circuits and fed by leaking gas from broken pipes. The boom of explosions is heard miles away. Inside city hall the mayor and other municipal workers are sent reeling, yet the domed structure somehow remains standing. Firefighters mobilize quickly, but their trucks cannot pass through the torn-up, rubble-strewn streets. Fire hydrants are all but useless because so many water mains have been severed by the tremors.

Much of the waterfront collapses under the shaking. Some expensive apartment houses, built on top of loose landfill, topple like so many dominoes. Hundreds of residents are killed or injured. As the ground sinks, the chilly waters of San Francisco Bay spill through low-lying residential streets.

There are scenes of carnage and chaos everywhere. The powerful vibrations break apart one elevated section of the Embarcadero Freeway. As the road crumbles, dozens of cars and trucks drop to the ground. A massive landslide buries the northern approaches to the Golden Gate Bridge, along with the vehicles on them. The great span itself begins to whip like an agitated snake but miraculously does not snap. The Bay Bridge also holds up, although its approaches collapse. In the avalanche of steel and concrete, many more vehicles are demolished. Completely isolated from the outside world, hundreds of subway riders are caught in the terrifying darkness of the swaying 3.6-mile-long BART tunnel linking San Francisco and Oakland under the bay.

Less than a minute has passed since the first jolt, but San Francisco already has the look of a ruin. Roadways are ripped apart or heaved up, railroad tracks have been twisted into surreal forms, numerous small bridges are broken hulks. At San Francisco International Airport, the runways look like washboards, the control tower has fallen, and numerous planes have become flaming heaps of scrap. In the main terminal hundreds of dazed travelers are staggering about with no hope of leaving.

In Oakland, where there are block after block of old frame dwellings, whole neighborhoods are ablaze. On the docks, giant steel cranes topple as if they were made of matchsticks. In Richmond, north of San Francisco, millions of gallons of oil and gasoline pour from storage tanks and pipes along the waterfront, creating ugly black slicks in the bay. To the south, entire hillsides fall into the Crystal Springs reservoirs; located directly astride the San Andreas fault, they are actually lakes created by its violent movements in the past. As the level of water rises, so does the pressure on the nineteenth-century dam holding it back. Eventually, the old structure fails, sending a 30-foot-high tidal wave of water rushing toward San Mateo and the posh homes of Hillsborough.

In Daly City, massive chunks of soft earth are shaken loose from cliffs and tumble into the Pacific Ocean. They carry with them dozens of suburban houses foolishly built atop these precarious perches. Hundreds of people are doomed. Elsewhere in the small communities near San Francisco, single-family homes rock wildly and their interiors become a hailstorm of flying shards of glass and crockery. But the frame construction of these dwellings holds them together, leaving most standing. The main casualties are older brick buildings, including a number of hospitals and schools, which do not have the lateral strength to resist the shaking.

The sickening motion seems to go on forever, nearly four endless minutes of shaking. Survivors are stunned. All around them lie the rubble and ruin of the earth's violence. Some cry hysterically. Others are too shocked and dazed to do anything. Children stumble through the streets calling for missing parents. Out of the wreckage of collapsed buildings come the moans and cries of the injured. The devastation seems beyond belief.

Rescue services struggle to overcome the most incredible obstacles. Poisonous gases are seeping out of broken pipes. Drinking water has become dangerously contaminated. At least half the city's telephones are dead. Many local radio and television stations have been silenced as well, increasing the difficulty of reaching or reassuring a major part of the distraught population. In dozens of buildings fires are roaring out of control. Even when firefighters can battle their way to them, many are allowed to go on burning for lack of water; the limited emergency supplies in special cisterns must be saved for drinking. Hundreds of people remain imprisoned in the infernos with no hope of escape. Some leap off balconies to their deaths.

The outside world mobilizes to ease San Francisco's plight, but the city is almost totally cut off. Roads are virtually impassable. Almost all of Route 101 south of Candlestick Park is awash under several feet of water. Other major highways are buried by landslides or blocked by gaps in the concrete as wide as 15 feet. Railroad tracks and airport runways are too badly damaged to be of any use. Only boats or helicopters can get doctors, nurses, or badly needed medical supplies into the city. Hours go by before assistance arrives in any significant quantity.

The area's own resources are pitifully limited. Half of its hospitals have been destroyed. Many hundreds of patients and medical workers, including doctors and nurses, have been killed. The surviving hospitals are barely able to take care of their own patients, to say nothing of the thousands of newly injured. Most of the city's emergency stores of drugs and other medical supplies have been lost. Precious blood plasma is rapidly spoiling because refrigerators stopped working after the power failures.

Small aftershocks continue to hit the area, knocking down buildings already weakened by the initial jolts. The quake's survivors are too frightened to go back into their homes. As they mill in the streets, they must rely on police loudspeakers and transistor radios for news from distant stations. Despite reassurances that state officials are organizing an intensive relief effort, there are wild rumors of major quakes hitting other metropolitan areas, of outbreaks of disease and rioting. It will be a long while before there is a semblance of sanity again.

After darkness closes in, the hapless crowds of people become increasingly despondent. Raging fires illuminate the night. No one is yet making any serious effort to dig out survivors trapped under the collapsed buildings. There are isolated incidents of looting. Screaming people engulf a Red Cross van demanding food and blankets. A few of the elderly scratch at the ruins of their houses for some prized possessions. Some people seek comfort in the handful of churches that have survived the earth's violence.

More than a week will pass before all the injured and homeless are found, tended to, and evacuated. Day after day, television newscasts carry grim images of the battered city. As the nation becomes aware of the full extent of San Francisco's agony, there is an outpouring of sympathy and support. Millions of dollars in food and clothing flood into the city. The president asks Congress to allocate a special emergency fund for rebuilding. Even so, it will take years before the proud metropolis, Baghdad on the Bay, as some like to call it, recovers from the quake. The final toll is more than 10,000 dead, at lease 300,000 injured, and property damage exceeding $10 billion.

This story of devastation is fictional. But it is one that could someday come true. No one can say when it will happen, or how extensive the damage will be, not even the seers and mystics who are forever proclaiming their special abilities to foretell the future. Yet virtually every earth scientist of repute is convinced that a major earthquake is a distinct possibility in San Francisco or, indeed, in many of the other populated areas along California's great seismic divide, the San Andreas fault.

Their predictions are not idle guesses. They grow out of studies of California's tremor-riddled history, which show that major quakes seem to have occurred at a rate of about one every century. This is not an exact figure, only an approximation based on a very incomplete reconstruction of California's seismic record. But even with their obvious gaps, the studies contain an ominous hint. In the San Francisco area, the San Andreas's last major upheaval occurred in 1906. If that event is taken as a marker, it suggests that Northern California's next major jolt should take place no later than the early years of the next century.

But as scientists who have tried to forecast quakes know only too well, the earth does not behave with anything like clockwork regularity. Its behavior is intricate, complex, and often baffling. For these reasons, the prediction of quakes, like handicapping horse races, remains a difficult and elusive art. Nonetheless, if California's past is any guide, scientists can be reasonably certain about one thing: the risk of a major quake along the San Andreas or associated faults rises with each passing year that one does not occur.

The seismic sword hangs not only over San Francisco and its

environs but over other regions as well, especially Los Angeles, where a major quake is also long overdue. If it occurred at the end of a business day, the devastation would be at least as widespread as in the mythical San Francisco quake, perhaps more so. A deadly preview of such a disaster very nearly unfolded on February 9, 1971, when a quake rocked the San Fernando Valley, north of Los Angeles. Though it was hardly a major temblor as earthquakes go, it cost 59 lives and did some $500 million in damage. Most of the deaths occurred in the collapse of a Veterans Administration hospital building that was thought to be quake proof. In another hospital two patients died when a power failure stopped their respirators. Other victims were crushed in their homes and in the collapse of a freeway overpass.

But the tragedy could have been even worse. The quake severely damaged a huge earthen dam overlooking the heavily populated valley. Only a few more seconds of shaking probably would have brought the barrier down. A great wall of water would have been released, swamping hundreds of one-family houses built in the shadow of the dam. Tens of thousands of lives might have been lost.

Most Americans assume that in the United States, at least, the blockbuster earthquake is wholly a California phenomenon, almost as indigenous to the state as surfboards, cults, and Jacuzzis. History does not bear them out. Major quakes have battered the East and Midwest as well and presumably will again. In 1755 a strong quake frightened Boston and other parts of New England. During the winter of 1811–1812, three exceptionally powerful temblors struck southeastern Missouri in rapid succession around the town of New Madrid. On August 31, 1886, a powerful quake shook Charleston, South Carolina. Quakes also recur frequently in the Saint Lawrence River Valley in upstate New York, along the Canadian border. Even the skyscrapers of

A highway overpass is a casualty of a quake that nearly brought disaster to California's San Fernando Valley in 1971.

Manhattan may be subject to the shakes. The lower part of that rock-ribbed island vibrated so severely one day in 1893 that billiard balls scattered in the pool halls of Greenwich Village. And just north of New York City, nuclear power plants sit less than a mile from a fault that seismologists say could rock them severely at almost any time. In spite of their vulnerability, however, these areas have taken even fewer precautions than California has to cope with the quake threat.

Belatedly recognizing that the United States had been dangerously lax in its earthquake preparations, the federal govern-

- Major
- Moderate
- Minor
- No risk

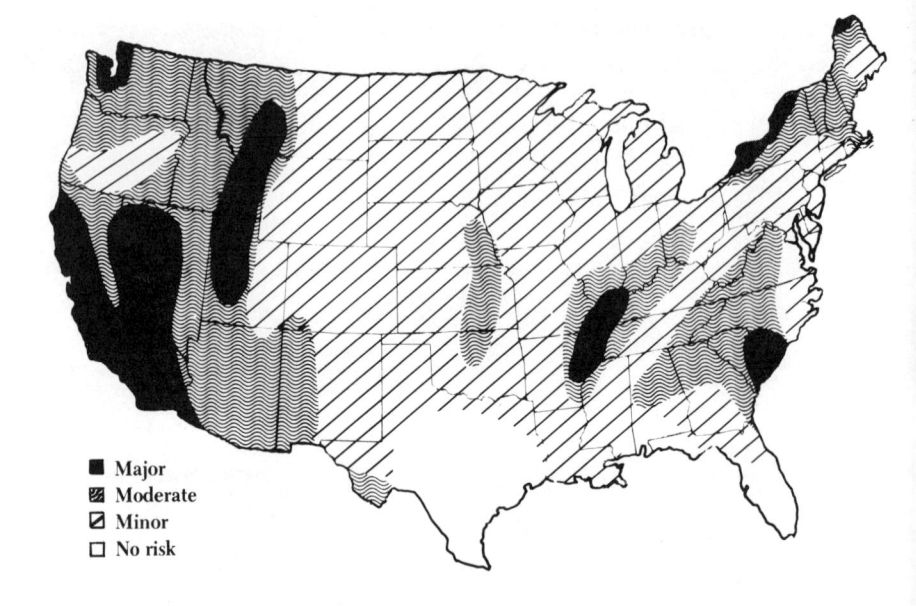

The various degrees of seismic risk in the continental United States based on historic records of past quakes.

ment began to allocate more money for seismic research in the early 1970s. It also attempted to stimulate greater awareness of quake dangers. As part of this effort, leading earthquake specialists were asked to calculate, as just one instructive example, what might happen to the San Francisco area if it were hit by a quake of the magnitude of the 1906 event. (Equally alarming studies have examined what might happen if large shocks hit Los Angeles.) The findings of the scientists varied depending on the exact time, intensity, and location of the hypothetical quake. But the experts agreed on a central point: if the earth unleashed its full fury on a working day, in the midst of the rush hour, the consequences would be far worse than those of any quake in United States history.

The Day That San Francisco Died

Such a quake would be a calamity not unlike a nuclear attack. The dead and injured would number in the hundreds of thousands. Tens of thousands more would be left homeless. Many older buildings would collapse, but so too would quite a few modern structures because they had been recklessly sited on dangerous ground. The losses would add up to many billions of dollars. It would pale even the great 1906 San Francisco quake, which took 700 lives and cost $400 million in property losses, mostly because of the fires that raged out of control after the initial shocks.

Fourth Street in Anchorage, Alaska, shows the scars of the earth's might following Alaska's 1964 Good Friday quake.

The enormous toll in this "worst case" scenario staggers the mind. It also raises troubling questions about public responsiveness to the earthquake risk. In recent years, engineers and builders have made enormous progress in their ability to design structures that can resist the motions of the most powerful quake. But the lessons of the drawing board have not always been put into practice. Since San Francisco was almost erased from the map in 1906, it has been rebuilt and expanded with a distressing blindness to the dangers of another major jolt. The proud new financial district has risen largely from land snatched from the bay. Fill is notoriously susceptible to shaking: strong vibrations can quickly turn it into a soft mush unable to support the structures sitting on top of it. San Francisco International Airport occupies such unstable ground that many experts feel it will not even withstand a quake of moderate severity. In Daly City, a bedroom town just south of San Francisco, thousands of new homes have been erected almost directly on the San Andreas fault. Some are perched so precariously close to the edge of eroding cliffs overlooking the Pacific that houses periodically tumble into the sea after only a heavy rain. A strong shock might cause an avalanche of dwellings.

Fortunately, the adoption of new quake-oriented building codes by the communities of the San Francisco area makes such reckless construction far less likely in the future. Public officials have also stepped up disaster-preparedness programs, storing food and medical supplies, working out evacuation procedures, and ensuring enough water for firefighting. But popular consciousness of the earthquake danger seems far from overwhelming. In and around San Francisco, geology professors from local colleges can often be seen leading their students through the streets, pointing out especially poorly located buildings, vulnerable walls, the sinking of the ground, and such signs of slow fault

The Day That San Francisco Died

movements as curbstones that no longer line up and roads that are slightly pulled to the side. Local residents seem totally indifferent to these quake tours or the gloomy message of the tour guides.

On one such scientific excursion, joined by the author, the group stopped in front of an old wooden house that had been erected directly across a spur of the San Andreas. The creeping movements of the fault were literally pulling the structure apart. Floors tilted, walls were askew, and the frames of doors and windows were badly twisted. The ramshackle building looked like a prop from a horror film. When the mistress of this seismic landmark was asked how she felt about being a regular stop on these quake tours, she reflected a moment, then replied, "Oh, I guess I'm used to it."

The calculations of likely damage in a future quake are all the more grim because they were not simply speculative exercises of the sort scientists sometimes churn out of a computer just for the fun of it. Rather, they are part of an attempt to begin confronting the earthly forces that cause quakes, forces as inexorable as the ocean's tides.

In the months and years before a quake, enormous pressures slowly build in the earth. Rocks are squeezed and pushed almost as if they were caught in a giant vise. The terrestrial engines at work here are so powerful that they can—indeed, do—move continents. Even the sturdiest bedrock is a mere plaything in their grip.

As the vise tightens, the rock comes closer and closer to the breaking point. Finally, succumbing to the strain, it snaps, suddenly and violently, like a plank of wood cracking under too much weight or the abrupt uncoiling of a clock spring that has been overwound. Yet these humble comparisons cannot really do justice to such a terrestrial tantrum. In an instant, the original fracture begins spreading. Billions of tons of bedrock lurch apart, tearing up everything in the path of the break. The rupture shudders the ground for miles around. Trees are knocked down. Buildings crumble. A deafening rumble fills the air. Even placid rivers and lakes are wildly stirred. This is an earthquake.

The forces at work in the earth are beyond anything in ordinary human experience. A quake of only modest strength releases 100 times as much energy as a Hiroshima-type atomic bomb. When a powerful earthquake struck Chile in May 1960, it sent the ground lurching more than 60 feet. Afterward, scientists discovered that the whole earth was ringing like a bell. Sometimes the oscillations from a big quake will continue for many weeks, possibly months. But an earthquake's physical effects can merely hint at the terror they induce in living things. Long before the shaking becomes apparent to humans, the keen senses of animals seem able to pick up hints of the impending upheaval. There are numerous reports of prequake animal terror—of rats fleeing into the streets, horses behaving skittishly in their stalls, gulls flying out to sea, snakes waking unexpectedly from midday slumber. No one knows how this early-warning ability of animals really works, but some scientists are talking of using it to sound quake alerts for humans.

Nothing could be more welcome than a reliable way to foretell quakes. In all of human experience, there is no sensation quite like the sudden, uncontrollable swaying of terra firma. Apart from the danger to life and property, there is the sheer terror of it all. Few people have described their reactions to an earthquake better than the evolutionist Charles Darwin, who experienced one in Chile in 1835 during his voyage aboard the *Beagle*. Darwin was ashore collecting fossils when the ground starting shaking so badly he had to lie down until the tremors stopped. Although Darwin was not injured, the quake and the following tsunami, or giant sea wave, killed some 5,000 people. In his journal, Darwin later wrote:

> A bad earthquake at once destroys our oldest associations; the earth, the very emblem of solidity, has moved beneath our feet like a thin crust over a fluid; one second of time has created in the mind a strange idea of insecurity, which hours of reflection would not have produced.

The slow, silent, underground tug-of-war that precedes the earth's rampages is not at all obvious to the casual eye. The gradual accumulation of stresses and strains within the rock can only be measured by the precise tools of seismology, the scientific study of earthquakes. But the might of the forces involved is clearly visible in the twisted and warped layers of rock exposed at cliffsides and by highway cuts, and in the ripping and scarring of the landscape along an active fault like the San Andreas, which has been the site of innumerable quakes. These provide tangible displays of their power to reshape the face of the earth.

Understanding of these forces has advanced considerably in recent years, so that hopes are high that someday perhaps scientists will be able to forecast quakes as easily as the weather. Indeed, there have already been some astonishingly accurate predictions—of when, where, and even with what force an earthquake will strike. But the spectacular successes have been matched by equally notable failures.

On a blustery, cold afternoon, February 4, 1975, party officials in the Chinese city of Haicheng (population: 100,000), located on the crowded Liaoning Province in Manchuria, ordered a prompt evacuation of all homes, shops, offices, and factories. Seismologists had detected ominous signs. That evening, while people sat huddled outdoors or in makeshift shelters, the anticipated shock came. It devastated the city and surrounding towns. The accurate forecast and quick response to it saved thousands of lives. But a year and a half later, the Chinese forecasters were caught by surprise. On July 28, 1976, two powerful shocks jolted the industrial and mining center of Tangshan, a city of more than a million only 100 miles east of the capital, Peking. Though the Chinese never made public official figures, the earthquake was one of the most costly in history. It appeared to have killed as many as 750,000 people. Foreign visitors said that the devastation was so total it reminded them of Hiroshima after the atomic bomb was dropped on it. For miles around, all that they could see was the rubble of homes and factories, the twisted remains of bridges and railroad tracks, and great piles of debris. No disaster quite like it had befallen China since the sixteenth century, when another massive tremor took more than 800,000 lives.

Can such disasters be averted in the future? Possibly. As seismologists learn more about the mechanisms of earthquakes, their predictions should become more reliable and more precise. But with this new skill will come new responsibilities for the scientists, to say nothing of the government and public. In a controlled society like China, it is relatively easy for officials to demand that citizens abandon quake-prone areas. But would an orderly evacuation be possible in crowded American cities? Or would an earthquake warning create widespread panic, or perhaps even indifference and cynicism? Just before the last appearance of Halley's comet in 1910, when some scientists warned that the earth might be enveloped in a cloud of deadly gases from the heavenly body's tail, some people responded with a round of mocking End of the World parties. Of course, it is a little harder to avoid an encounter with a comet than an earthquake. But even if citizens would heed an evacuation call, would it be practical or possible to evacuate a major city like Los Angeles before the quake struck? At the very least, the task of getting people out of crowded metropolitan areas would require extensive preparations long in advance of any disaster.

Some scientists are considering an even more dramatic way of dealing with quakes. By artificially triggering a series of small quakes, they hope to relieve the strain that could produce a single large quake. Already there have been small-scale experiments showing that the scheme seems to have some practical potential. But it is also one that poses unquestionable risks. If the test misfired, it could cause the very quake it was designed to avert. Should scientists be allowed to go ahead with the experiments in spite of the danger? If they were given permission, who would be responsible for any damage that might ensue?

Such are the thorny questions raised by the advances in seismology. Not too long ago it was an obscure science, one rarely in the public eye, except when a quake occurred. Now that is changing. By shedding new light on the age-old forces at work within the earth—and finally offering some means to contain them—seismology has moved into the very forefront of the earth sciences. And with that success have come both problems and opportunities for seismology's practitioners.

2 OXEN, CATFISH, AND ANGRY GODS

In ancient Japan, people believed that the earth was borne on the back of a giant spider. As the creature bestirred itself, perhaps out of anger or as it rose from slumber, its powerful movements shook the entire earth and its occupants. In this colorful way, the Japanese explained the frequent earthquakes that beset their nation of islands.

Later the beast that carried the terrestrial burden became a catfish, or namazu. According to Japanese storytellers, the namazu was so prone to pranks that it had to be watched over by a god, who was called the Kashima. To remind the fish to be on its best behavior, he always held a mallet in his hand. But at times the Kashima god's attention was diverted from these duties, and the namazu could thrash about to its heart's content, shaking the earth as much as it wanted to.

Even as recently as 1855 some Japanese still clung to the old superstition. In October of that year a powerful quake rocked Tokyo (then known as Edo), killing many people. The calamity occurred during the legendary "month without gods" when the heavenly lords were thought to be off at a remote shrine, leaving the catfish by itself to do its mischief. For those citizens of Edo

Japanese print shows the Kashima, seated, ordering the pounding of the legendary namazu, whose shaking was thought to be responsible for earthquakes, as a warning to onlooking namazu.

who believed in the myth, the quake was proof that the Kashima was indeed needed to keep the namazu from playing deadly tricks. To this day, some Japanese still like to display decorative prints of the namazu and the god on the walls of their homes in hopes of getting a little extra protection against quakes.

The Japanese were not alone in inventing such quaint tales to explain earthquakes. In ancient times, many people believed that the earth rode on the back of a great animal, but there was considerable disagreement about what sort of creature it was. A fidgety fish, for example, would not do for the Chinese, who also reside in one of the earth's more tremor-prone regions. They said that the earth's cantankerous behavior was due to a mighty ox, a belief they shared with some of the peoples of ancient Arabia and Africa. As the ox ambled along, shifting its terrestrial load from side to side, the earth was jostled.

The Mongolians, dwelling beyond China's Great Wall in the deserts to the northwest, thought the culprit was an oversized hog. So did the people of the Celebes, an island chain in the South Pacific. The Sumatrans, who occupy still another Pacific island, blamed a giant crab; the Persians, a dragon. The Indians (of India, not America) variously chose an elephant or a mole. Across the seas, some of their namesakes in North America, the Algonquins, believed the earth sat on the hard-shelled back of a giant tortoise, while the Indians of South America were convinced it was carried bumpily along on the broad shoulders of a whale.

Recounted by a village elder around a campfire, these spirited tales may have had entertainment value in their day, just as did the stories the ancients told about the gods and goddesses who inhabited the starry constellations. But the legends also filled another need. They helped explain what surely must have been—and certainly still is—an event of utmost terror: the sudden, unexpected movement of the ground.

The idea that the earth was transported by giant animals is also intriguing for other reasons. It suggests that the ancients understood, if only in a primitive way, that the earth was a distinct celestial entity, perhaps a sphere, and that somehow it whirled across the heavens. But this interpretation of the stories credits the ancients with a view of the universe that is too modern and sophisticated. In fact, their cosmology was quite simple. Most of them regarded the earth as fixed in place, supported by some giant beast or a figure like Atlas, the titan of Greek myth who, as punishment for revolting against the gods, was compelled to hold up the heavens. In this picture of the universe, the earth occupies center stage; even if they were regarded as the abode of the gods, the sun, moon, planets, and stars were all distinctly secondary players.

Nowadays we can smile tolerantly at such seemingly naive ideas, smugly comfortable in our superior world view. For us, images of the earth, photographed from space by satellites and voyaging astronauts, have become almost an everyday sight. But the ancients, unable to climb higher than a mountaintop, except in their mind's eye, had no such global perspective. Nor did they have the tools or the scientific skills to understand the strange, lurching movements of the ground that seemed to strike without warning or reason. What they did have, however, were lively imaginations and a rich storytelling tradition.

One old legend among the native people of Siberia's chilly Kamchatka Peninsula holds that quakes occurred when a mighty dog named Kozei shook freshly fallen snow off his furry coat. (A slightly less romantic version of this story has sled dogs scratching themselves to get rid of fleas.) In another local legend, quakes are generated by a god named Tuli, who drove a sled under the earth. Only loud shouts, noisemaking, or symbolic jabbing of the air with a pestle could scare him off and dispel the earthquake threat. On the Siberian mainland, the discovery of the remains of many giant mammoths led to a different theory. People there believed that the huge beasts dwelled underground and shook the earth when they stomped about.

The Babylonians, who were the world's first serious stargazers, felt heavenly bodies controlled all natural events. Their ideas marked the beginnings of astrology, the pseudoscientific ancestor of astronomy. In the Babylonian scheme of things, earthquakes were caused by three "wandering stars," or planets, Jupiter, Saturn, and Mars, all of them divinities with rather violent tempers.° If they were sufficiently annoyed by events on earth, these celestial gods could also hurl down a thunderbolt or two.

The early Greeks saw earthquakes as the tantrums of the sea god Poseidon, better known to us by his Roman name, Neptune. In Greek mythology, Poseidon used his familiar triple-pronged spear to control the waves of the sea, to break rocks and boulders, and to rattle the coastline. On one occasion Poseidon was angered by the disobedient giant Polybotes, who refused to heed the gods. Chasing him across the Aegean Sea, Poseidon set off quakes wherever he put down his galloping feet. When he finally cornered the upstart on Kos, Poseidon ripped off a chunk of the island and hurled it at him. Polybotes was buried under a mountain of debris. To appease their hot-tempered sea god and prevent his earthshaking rampages, the Greeks worshipped Poseidon in ceremonies along the shore and in special temples dedicated to him.

As inhabitants of an area frequently devastated by quakes and volcanic eruptions, the Greeks had every reason to believe that the mysterious disasters were the whim of the gods. Nonetheless, they were also the first people to try to explain them in a nonmythical, or scientific, way, attributing them to natural causes rather than the misbehavior of unpredictable beasts. In this effort, however, they were bound to fail, since they lacked a basic understanding of the earth and did not have the instru-

---

°A modern version of this theory has been dubbed the Jupiter Effect. It holds that when the massive planets Jupiter and Saturn are lined up with the earth and other planets, more or less like a column of soldiers, on one side of the sun, as they were early in 1982, the added gravitational pull would disturb the sun, starting a chain of events ultimately triggering earthquakes. But there was no noticeable rise in quakes during this period. Nor have scientists found any indication in the historical record of an increase in quakes when similar planetary lineups took place in the past. For this reason, they almost unanimously reject the theory, even though its authors still insist it contains more than a grain of truth.

ments that would have enabled them to begin gaining this knowledge. But they did make a number of shrewd observations about the troubling terrestrial phenomena. They noted, for example, that earthquakes were often followed by so-called tidal waves, or what today's scientists call tsunamis, Japanese for "storm waves." As the ancient Greeks suspected, such waves are triggered not by tides but by earthquakes on the sea floor.

Several Greek philosophers suggested physical mechanisms for the earth's rumblings. Anaxagoras (circa 500–428 B.C.), a friend of the great Athenian orator Pericles, believed that within the earth there was a blazing fire. When this natural furnace was stoked, the escaping vapors shook the earth and caused quakes. Aristotle, who lived in the fourth century B.C. and was the most famous thinker of ancient Greece, believed that winds were drawn into the earth's interior, where they fanned the underground fires. As the hot vapors from the flames swirled about and tried to escape, they rattled the earth. The explanation was in accord with the Greek view that the universe was composed of four basic elements: earth, air, fire, and water. The philosopher Strabo (64 B.C. to about A.D. 21) went on to fit volcanoes into Aristotle's theory. He described them as a kind of safety valve for releasing the pent-up underground winds hypothesized by Aristotle.

Here was another clever guess by the ancients. In recent years, scientists have discovered that there is in fact a link between quakes and volcanoes, but the connection is quite different from that imagined by Strabo. The Greek who seems to have come closest to modern ideas about quakes was Anaximenes, who taught as early as the sixth century B.C. that they occurred when masses of rock deep in the earth collided with great force. Still, some of ancient Greece's sages preferred to cling to mystical explanations. Pythagoras, who also lived in the sixth century B.C.

and was a believer in the magical power of numbers, said that the earth shook when the dead fought among themselves.

The Romans, who eventually conquered the Greeks, also helped themselves to the best of their thought, including their theories about quakes. The poet Lucretius (circa 96–55 B.C.), in what sounds like a repetition of Anaximenes, blamed the movement of underground rock. The Roman naturalist and encyclopedist Gaius Plinius Secundus, better known as Pliny the Elder, preferred the Aristotelian view. He wrote that "tremors never occur except when the sea is calm and the sky so still that birds are unable to soar." And why was this so? Because, said Pliny, echoing Aristotle, "the veins and hidden hollows of the sky" drew all the breath out of the air before a quake and piped them into the ground. Pliny said that they did the same thing before unleashing a lightning bolt.

This concept gave rise to the notion that earthquakes are often preceded by a stuffiness in the air. Even today the idea of "earthquake weather" still lingers in many quake-prone parts of the world, and some people insist they can "feel" when a quake is about to hit, just as some say that they can tell in their bones when rain will come. In fact, scientists now suspect that subtle atmospheric changes do sometimes precede quakes and perhaps could serve as an early-warning signal. But such portents were of no help to poor Pliny. His life ended at age 56, apparently of a heart attack, while the portly, puffing philosopher was trying to flee one of the major natural disasters of the ancient world: the unexpected eruption of Mount Vesuvius, which buried the thriving Roman towns of Pompeii and Herculaneum in a shower of volcanic ash in the year A.D. 79.

For all the death and destruction caused by quakes, a few people like the Carib Indians could look on them in a favorable light. Among these early conquerors of the Antilles, the volcanic islands of the Caribbean basin, there was a saying that earthquakes meant Mother Earth was dancing and bidding all her children to take part in the festivities. The Carib, who came from the Amazon jungles, had a special reputation for ferocity. In the early fourteenth century, they wrested the Antilles from their original inhabitants, the peaceful Arawak Indians, whose civilization they destroyed. After a battle, the Carib indulged in the ritual eating of the bodies of their victims. To the first Spanish explorers of the Antilles, the very name Carib evoked fear and became the Spanish word for cannibalism. Even so, the belligerence of the Carib did not save them. A few centuries later, they were themselves wiped out by the Spanish.

Yet the most common attitude toward earthquakes has always been that they are a sign of heavenly anger. Through the ages rulers have taken special precautions against incurring divine wrath. In the sixth century, the Byzantine emperor Justinian prohibited swearing (including by the hair of one's head), blasphemy, and other acts he deemed ungodly, one of which was public kissing. Justinian felt such behavior was a sure invitation to earthquakes. In the seventeenth century, a Belgian chemist named J. B. van Helmont explained how a punitive God might unleash quakes. He said that at God's behest, an avenging angel struck a heavenly bell. Its vibrations shook the atmosphere, which in turn violently agitated the ground.

Such views prevailed as late as 1750, when a mild earthquake was felt in London, a city that had experienced slight tremors only once in the preceding 200 years. It did nothing more than shake windows and rattle cupboards, but preachers sounded an alarm. "O, that our repentence may prevent heavier marks of His displeasure," wrote the Methodist leader John Wesley in his journal.

Exactly four weeks later, London felt that displeasure. The English capital was jolted by a second and much more powerful quake that rang bells, knocked down chimneys, tumbled some buildings, and threw the city into a religious tizzy. On the subsequent Sunday, churches were packed with frightened worshippers. The Reverend Doctor Thomas Sherlock, bishop of London, sternly told members of his flock that the quakes were very clear warnings to repent their sins. Many Londoners fled to the countryside lest they be caught in a still more destructive upheaval. At least one sage forecast the end of the world. Recalling the panic years later in a letter to a friend, Wesley wrote: "There is no divine visitation which is likely to have so general an influence on sinners as an earthquake." Sinners surely had plenty to worry about that year. In the following months, the British Isles were jostled by three more quakes. They did no real damage, but 1750 became enshrined forever in English history as "the year of earthquakes."

If the mid-century tremors rattled England's unfaithful, there were far greater reverberations from a quake that struck Portugal five years later on November 1, 1755, All Saints' Day. Before the disaster was over, Lisbon, the proud capital of a great empire, a bastion of Catholicism, a city of commerce and culture, lay in ruins. As Lisbon crumbled, so did many of the basic assumptions of Western thought.

The quake was one of the great natural calamities in history. It began on a crisp, sunny autumn morning when Lisbon's many churches were packed with the devout who had come to honor the saints and the blessed in heaven. Suddenly, at 9:40 A.M., the worshippers heard a loud, rumbling noise. Walls started to sway and chandeliers began to swing wildly overhead. As the ground's motion continued, sacramental objects tumbled off pulpits, windows shattered, and cracks opened in the sides of buildings. In Lisbon's crowded harbor, a sea captain watched with increasing horror as the city's stately old stone buildings, erected on terraced hillsides overlooking the River Tagus, began to rock omi-

The 1755 Lisbon quake, dramatically shown in this old engraving, also shook the underpinnings of Western thought.

nously back and forth—"like a wheat field in a breeze," he later recalled.

Clutching their rosaries and missals, the terrified worshippers fled the Basilica de Santa Maria, Lisbon's ancient cathedral. Flocking into the narrow square in front of the basilica, many sank to their knees. While they prayed aloud, imploring God to spare them, they were joined by people fleeing other churches and nearby houses. Within minutes, the square was a crowded, screaming mass of frightened humanity.

Forty minutes later, while most of the city still reeled from the first round of trembling, Lisbon was struck by an even more powerful shock. Buildings already weakened by the first tremors came crashing to earth. The damage was especially severe in the jammed square in front of the basilica. As chunks of masonry fell, a great cloud of dust rose, cloaking the horrifying scene. When the pall lifted, the basilica was gone, as were neighboring buildings. The square itself had become a heap of rubble and a graveyard for almost everyone in it.

But the earth had yet another horror in store for Lisbon. After the first shock, hundreds of people sought safety on a gleaming new marble quay recently built on the banks of the River Tagus. With the quake's initial movements, the river receded, exposing the bottom all the way out to a sandbar at the Tagus's mouth. But as the tremors started again, or perhaps a few moments before—the recollections of survivors differed—the river swept back in a 50-foot-high wave that washed over the quay and carried off all the people on it. Twice more there were big surges of water, each time trapping more people as well as small boats in deadly whirlpools.

Then came Lisbon's ultimate ordeal. During the first round of shaking, fires had been ignited all over the city. Toppling over on church altars, candles set pews and tapestries ablaze. In private homes and palaces, timbers from collapsing roofs fell onto kitchen hearths, sending sparks flying in all directions. As the people ran into the streets, they ignored the fires, which spread rapidly and soon engulfed the city in a single, uncontrollable inferno. It raged for three days, fanned by a steady northeasterly wind. When the flames at last died out, the destruction was total. Even those structures that had survived the earth's most violent shaking succumbed to the fire.

The final reckoning was staggering. As many as 60,000 people were killed, nearly a quarter of Lisbon's population. Many of the victims were the faithful, crushed in the fall of stones and timber while they were at prayer. Some were buried alive. Others died from severe burns. For days after the dreadful morning, priests raced about the city giving last rites. More than 9,000 buildings were destroyed. In Lisbon's ruins lay magnificent palaces and churches, including the royal residence and an opera house completed only eight months earlier. Also incinerated were warehouses filled with silks and spices, archives containing thousands of books and manuscripts chronicling Portuguese exploration and trade, and collections of priceless paintings, including works by such masters as Rubens, Correggio, and Titian.

But damage was not limited to Portugal. The tremors were so strong that they were felt in much of Europe and North Africa. In Luxembourg, some 500 soldiers died when a barracks collapsed. The shocks and ocean waves killed some 10,000 people in Morocco; the city of Algiers was almost totally wrecked. As far north as Scandinavia, rivers and lakes inexplicably overflowed their banks. In the English county of Derbyshire, nearly 1,000 miles from the quake's center, plaster fell off walls and a fissure opened in the ground. While he was giving a sermon, a minister in Scotland felt his church rock and his congregation suddenly tip to the side as if it were on the deck of a rolling ship.

The great quake also had a more subtle effect. Throughout the Western world, it prompted a new round of agonized soul-searching. Many Portuguese regarded Lisbon's destruction as an indication of God's anger with them. And English Protestants had no hesitation in providing reasons for that wrath. They noted that Lisbon had been a stronghold of the feared Inquisition, which enforced Roman orthodoxy under penalty of death, and the home of an empire that ruled conquered peoples, like the Indians of America, with a savage hand. To prevent a recurrence of the disaster, the learned men of the University of Coimbra are said to have recommended slowly burning a few sinners at the stake. (Some cynics might argue that there was merit in the idea, since no quake of importance has struck Portugal since then.) But most Portuguese reacted in a more sensible and civilized way, working rapidly to rebuild and restore the luster of their capital.

Much harder to repair was the psychological damage. Occurring during a period that had come to be known as the Enlightenment, or the Age of Reason, the calamity had a profound impact on the intellectual climate of the day. With only a few powerful shakes of the earth, European intellectuals were thoroughly jarred out of their prevailing optimism. The Lisbon quake undermined their faith in an orderly and understandable universe and severely tested their belief in a kindly, benevolent deity. All but buried by the Lisbon quake was the widely held notion that this was, in the sardonic words of the French satirist Voltaire, the "best of all possible worlds." Never before had the Age of Reason seen nature behave so unreasonably.

The French-Swiss philosopher Jean-Jacques Rousseau drew his own special lesson from the disaster. He saw it as vindication of his belief that man should live as close as possible to his "natural state." In a scolding schoolmaster's tone, he pointed out that if people had still lived outdoors, more of them might have survived the Lisbon quake.

There was also a positive consequence of Europe's earthquake activity: it spurred renewed scientific thinking about the phenomenon. Most scientists of the time, still under the influence of Aristotle, viewed earthquakes as a product of the ebb and flow of underground fluids and gases. A quaint summary of these ideas is given in William Caxton's 1480 work *Mirrour of the World*, one of the first encyclopedias published in English. He wrote that as subterranean streams compressed the air in underground caverns, winds would build up and shake the earth. If they were really powerful, they would push right through the surface, opening up a hole that might swallow a castle or even an entire city.

But after the latest European quakes, new ideas came forth. Breaking with past theories that quakes were the result of turbulent underground vapors, the English clergyman William Stukeley, who was also a medical doctor, ascribed them to electricity, then still something of a curiosity. He elaborated his contention before the august Royal Society in London and in a popular tome called *Philosophy of Earthquakes*. But in spite of the scientific sound of his work, the idea of a divine hand in the ground's rumblings was very much part of Stukeley's theorizing. The reverend doctor insisted that the quake-producing electricity was only an outward expression of God's will. How could it be otherwise? he asked. For this "chastening rod," as he called quakes, was directed against populated towns and cities, which he regarded as centers of sin, rather than the peaceful and sin-free countryside.

Stukeley neglected to note that earthquakes could easily go unobserved in less populated or uninhabited areas. Today we know that many, if not most, earthquakes occur on the ocean floor, far from anyplace where they can do much harm (except when they create destructive tsunamis). But Stukeley's speculations impressed his contemporaries. Similar ideas were heard as far away as the American colonies, where New Englanders gave them a special local twist: they wondered whether the "electrical substance" responsible for earthquakes might not be drawn out of the air by Benjamin Franklin's lightning rods. Franklin himself wrote, "If a nonelectric cloud discharges its contents on any part of the earth, when in a highly electrified state, an earthquake must necessarily ensue."

The colonists had a particular reason to fret. Only 17 days after the Lisbon disaster, in the early hours of the morning, powerful jolts awoke the residents of Boston, capital of the Massachusetts colony. Tremors were felt along hundreds of miles of the Atlantic coast from the Carolinas to Nova Scotia. While there are no reports of any human casualties, chimneys fell by the thousands, a large fissure opened in southern New Hampshire, dust spouted out of cracks along some beaches, and Boston's Faneuil Hall lost its famous gilded cricket weather vane. From the pulpits came another round of preaching about human wickedness, but at least one learned New Englander viewed the quake in what then must have seemed a shockingly different way.

When the shaking finally stopped, John Winthrop IV, an astronomer and mathematician at Harvard College, arose from his bed and immediately looked at his watch. By comparing its hands with those of a free-standing pendulum clock, which had been jolted to a halt by the first tremor, he reckoned that the quake lasted about three and a half minutes, a relatively long interval of shaking, as earth tremors go. He also tried to calculate the forces at work in the quake by measuring how far objects had been thrown by it. From their trajectories through the air, he realized that the quake struck from a northerly direction. And he was just about right: the quake originated off Cape Ann, which lies north of Boston.

His most significant insight, though, came a few days later, while he was sitting by his fireplace and some aftershocks vibrated the bricks. He noticed that they moved in sequence, one after another, almost like tumbling dominoes, rather than as a single entity. From this observation he realized that the shaking was caused, not by one large blow, but by a rolling, wavelike motion through the earth. He had discovered a characteristic of quakes that would eventually play a critical role in the ability of science to study them: they transmitted their energy in waves, not entirely unlike those of the sea. Some time later in a talk at the Harvard chapel, Winthrop went so far as to say that earthquakes were of "real and standing advantage to the globe" by opening up the pores of the earth just as a plough loosens the soil. That surely jolted his God-fearing colleagues at Harvard.

Also in 1755, a Benedictine monk named Benito Jeŕonimo Feyzóo y Montenegro, following a different line of thought, wondered whether quakes were caused by a gradual contracting of the earth. The idea was not entirely farfetched. By the middle of the eighteenth century, educated Europeans accepted the Copernican concept of the earth as a great rotating sphere that traveled in a fixed path around the sun. It was also suspected that the planet might still be slowly cooling off from what was presumed to be its fiery birth. Thus as the earth lost heat into space, it might also be shrinking. In the process, its outer skin would shrivel and crack, thereby causing earthquakes. The contraction idea was later championed by the nineteenth-century Austrian geologist Eduard Suess, who saw in it an explanation for many geological mysteries, including the building of mountains.

A year later, a Portuguese soldier named Miguel Tibéro Pedegache Brandão Ivo raised another intriguing possibility. He suggested that the moon and perhaps even the sun might have something to do with earthquakes. Though he did not specify exactly how these relationships worked, it was not a bad guess. Three-quarters of a century earlier, the English scientific genius Isaac Newton had shown that the old Babylonians were right, at least in a general way: the heavens *do* influence the earth. The heavenly hand is exercised through what he called the universal law of gravitation.

In a brilliant series of mathematical equations, Newton showed how celestial bodies are bound to each other by their mutual gravity. The strength of this attraction is directly proportional to the masses of the bodies (that is, the amount of matter they contain) and inversely proportional to the square of the distance between them. Therefore the bigger and closer they are, the greater the pull they exert on each other. One consequence of the particular interaction between the earth and moon is the daily ebb and flow of the tides. Thus if the moon's, or the sun's, gravity could raise water levels on earth, it might also be able to tug at the crust and cause a quake.

Much closer to the mark were the proposals of a lecturer and clergyman at England's Cambridge University named John Michell. Like Winthrop, he had a special interest in astronomy. But after the flurry of earthquakes, he devoted his considerable intellectual energies to trying to explain them. In 1760, five years after Lisbon's destruction, he published the results of his investigation in a landmark treatise that offered nothing less than a comprehensive theory of earthquakes.

Michell believed that earthquakes were caused by masses of shifting rock and linked these movements to underground fires. In this respect, his ideas were essentially no different than those of the ancient Greeks. What made his views distinctive, however, was his shrewd analysis of the motions that the quakes set off. He said they came in the form of two different types of waves. The first waves consisted of a "tremulous" or shaking motion; this was followed by a second series that moves with almost snakelike undulations. These two types of waves are very much like the basic seismic waves identified by modern seismologists. Michell also suggested a way of locating a quake's place of origin. He said that this could be done by taking a map of the general quake region and drawing lines to show the direction of the seismic waves as they arrive at different sites. Where these lines come together, if they are extended, indicates where the quake began. Michell's paper brought him election to the Royal Society, but shortly thereafter he resumed his study of astronomy and his novel ideas slipped into obscurity. Only many years later were they rediscovered and fully appreciated for their shrewd insights into earthquake behavior.

In spite of all the theorizing, however, earthquakes still remained a mystery. In some unfathomable way, powerful forces were being unleashed inside the earth. But what were these forces? And why did they strike at some times and not others? Such questions would continue to puzzle scientists for decades to come. Not until our own day would these earthly riddles finally be unraveled.

3 Rumbles in the Heartland

To the authors of the Old Testament, there was no sterner test of faith than remaining steadfast in the face of an earthquake. "Therefore will we not fear," say the Psalms, "though the earth be removed, and though the mountains be carried into the midst of the sea; though the waters thereof roar and be troubled, though the mountains shake with the swelling thereof."

Located in an area of great geological activity, ancient Palestine was hardly a stranger to the earth's rumblings. Quakes occurred often and with considerable violence. One Biblical allusion to them may be Moses's stormy ascent to the top of Mount Sinai to receive the tablets. Earthquakes also could have caused the collapse of the walls of Jericho; in fact, scientists have found evidence of tremors in the region during that period (about 1100 B.C.). Even those sinful cities Sodom and Gomorrah may have been the victims of quakes, although the Bible says only that they were destroyed by a divinely inspired heavenly fire.

In antiquity, earthquakes were not just a cruel fact of life and a sign of divine wrath. They were a puzzling obsession, recorded and commented upon by many writers. Pliny, for example, provided a lengthy, if second-hand, account of the destruction of 12 cities in Asia by strong tremors. Yet as earthquake observers—indeed, as observers of all natural phenomena—no one in the ancient world equaled the Chinese. Besides carefully noting astronomical events like the appearance of new stars, comets, and sunspots, they chronicled every quake of any destructive force dating back to the year 1831 B.C. Their diligent record-keeping has left us with a virtually uninterrupted inventory of nearly 3,000 years of earthquakes.

Because of these meticulously kept records, we know of the horrifying toll from a powerful earthquake that struck Shensi province in central China in 1556. Lists survive containing the names of some 820,000 people who were killed in the disaster. Still more victims may have gone unrecorded. In terms of loss of human life, the quake is the worst in history.

In Japan, perhaps the most quake-prone country on earth, the records date back to A.D. 416. But they have many gaps and are not nearly so complete as those kept by the Chinese. Not until the start of the seventeenth century did the Japanese begin keeping an unbroken chronology of major quakes.

Still, even though the Chinese were more diligent than their neighbors in recording natural phenomena, they did not do much theorizing about earthquakes. Unlike the Greeks and Romans, they felt that quakes, along with other mysteries of nature, were beyond human comprehension. And so the Chinese suffered them quietly and stoically, without really trying to do anything about them.

However, there was one early Chinese scholar by the name of Chang Heng—in some accounts he is called by the Japanese version of his name, Choko—who broke with this passive tradition. Considering the time in which he lived (A.D. 78–139), his insights into quakes were remarkable. It is clear from the unusual instrument he created that he thought about how earthquakes work and understood, at least intuitively, that they send waves through the ground, just as a pebble tossed into a pond gives off expanding ripples of water. He also realized that like these aquatic disturbances, the ground waves may travel a long way and shake objects in regions far from the place of the quake's origin.

But Chang Heng was not content just to speculate. To pick up the faint tremors of a distant quake, he designed an extraordinary device, the earliest ancestor of what we now know as the seismograph (from the Greek words for "shake" and "write"). By all accounts, Chang Heng's invention was not only ingeniously clever but, in the classic Chinese manner, crafted with much artistry and style.

The apparatus consisted of a large bronze vessel, perhaps as much as eight feet in diameter. Ringing its middle were eight

Model of Chang Heng's pioneering seismoscope, including cutaway view showing internal pendulum and levers. Ball would drop from a dragon's jaw into mouth of waiting frog in response to only faint tremors from far-off earthquake.

dragons' heads, spaced equal distances apart like the points on a compass rose. Each of the handcrafted beasts held a ball loosely in its jaws. Placed directly under the dragons, around the base of the vessel, were eight metal frogs, one under every dragon. They looked upward with their mouths wide open so they could catch any balls that might fall their way.

In the center of the big metal vat was a heavy pendulum, connected to a system of levers, which in turn could open or close the dragons' jaws. Slight vibrations of the ground barely perceptible to bystanders would start the pendulum swinging. If an earthquake occurred, even one a great distance away, the pendulum would move, opening a dragon's jaws and dropping a ball into the gaping mouth of one of the waiting frogs.

The device was not only a seismic detector but something of a quake direction finder as well. As the pendulum swung, it followed the same pathway as the traveling waves. Only a ball held in the jaws of a dragon perched directly along this route would be released. Thus the dragon that had lost a ball served in effect as a pointer facing in the direction of the quake.

Chang Heng did not have to stand watch constantly over his detector to see if a quake had occurred. The instrument operated entirely on its own. The pendulum was apparently so sensitive that it could react to tremors much too faint to be felt by human senses. All Chang Heng had to do was come around every so often to check if a ball had been knocked out of a dragon's mouth.

But did the gadget really work? Apparently it did, on at least one occasion. In the year A.D. 132, a ball tumbled suddenly into a frog's mouth, even though no one felt the ground shaking. Chang Heng's contemporaries scornfully brushed off the signal. In the absence of any noticeable vibrations, they refused to believe that there might have been a quake somewhere. Several days later, a horseman galloped into town from far away and breathlessly reported that his home area had been battered by a quake. It had taken place on the very day the ball dropped out of the dragon's mouth. What's more, the messenger came from the exact direction indicated by the dragon.

With that auspicious performance of his instrument, Chang Heng's reputation soared. He was no longer seen as an earthquake-obsessed eccentric, but as a man of true genius. His fame spread across the countryside, and he became the emperor's personal adviser on earthquakes—in a sense, the world's first official seismologist. Today scientists would call Chang Heng's colorful, if primitive, contraption a seismoscope, or simple earthquake detector, rather than a full-fledged seismograph, since it did not measure the strength of the earthquake waves, time their appearance, or leave behind any record other than the fallen ball. Of course, his success may have been just a bit of good luck. Some historians of science find it hard to believe that his ornamented pot could detect a quake, let alone determine its direction. In any event, whether it worked or not, nothing more is said about Chang Heng or his magical dragon vat in the old Chinese chronicles, and the idea of quake detectors seems to have been forgotten. Centuries passed before anyone tried to build a similar instrument.

In the New World, no written record of quakes predates the arrival of the Europeans. But Indian legends, passed down from one generation to the next by gifted tribal storytellers, are filled with references to the earth's ominous rumblings and the great beasts in its interior that were thought to be causing them. There are also more direct reminders of the earth's violent past. When geologists look at such things as fault lines, landslides, and the sharp, clifflike rises called scarps, they see in them vivid proof that the ground was rocked by earthquakes. Through careful study of such quake-torn terrain, some scientists have managed to identify exactly when ancient temblors took place (see Chapter 8).

Scientists have recently turned to a less direct way of finding out where and when quakes may have taken place in the distant past. The technique involves a relatively young science with the tongue-twisting name of dendrochronology (from the Greek words for "tree" and "time"), the dating of events and variations in environment through the study of tree rings. These are the circular layers of annual growth that the tree adds around its trunk, just under the bark, every year of its life.

By carefully counting the number of rings, scientists can tell exactly how old a particular tree may be. Some specimens of giant redwoods, Douglas firs, and bristlecone pines have been found to be hundreds and even thousands of years old. But antiquity alone is not what dendrochronologists are looking for. Rings grow at varying rates. Some years trees lay down thick rings. Other years there may be barely any new growth at all. How much material trees add any particular year depends on such environmental factors as the amount of rainfall, the average temperature, and the intensity of sunlight. To dendrochronologists, trees are a living window on the past, a kind of arboreal history book in which every ring acts as a separate page in the story. All sorts of priceless scientific information may be hidden away in these pages—about ancient climate, the level of solar radiation, even whether an earthquake has occurred near the trees.

For skilled practitioners of dendrochronology, reading the pages for clues to seismic history is relatively easy. When a powerful quake strikes a forested area, some trees will be knocked over and killed outright, while others may be left alive and well but slightly tilted. Like the colorful roly-poly Russian dolls that always land right side up when they are pushed, such trees have a natural inclination to return to an upright position. Almost immediately a tilted tree will start depositing more new growth material around its trunk in the direction of the lean than away from it. In other words, the tree tries to prop itself up.

Years later, when dendrochronologists examine a cross section of the trunk, the tree's effort at self-repair will still be visible. It will show up within the pattern of rings as a place where they have suddenly begun to fatten on one side and thin out on the other. Taken in conjunction with direct geological evidence in the area, this abnormality in the rings is a pretty good sign that the region was once hit by a quake. To tell when the quake struck, the scientists simply count back the number of rings added by the tree since the start of the uneven growth.

In this way scientists of the U.S. Geological Survey and the University of Arizona's tree ring research laboratory determined that a major quake had shuddered California's San Andreas fault in the northern part of the state around the year A.D. 1650. The information was inferred from the severe tilting of a group of old redwoods in Fort Ross State Park. Examination of two leaning Douglas firs near Gualala, in Mendocino County, indicated that still another quake had occurred in the area late in the eighteenth century.

Unlike many sciences dealing with living things, dendrochronology does not require the destruction of its test subjects. To obtain a cross section of a tree trunk, ecologically minded dendrochronologists do not saw down valuable old trees. Instead they use special boring tools to drill out pencil-thin cores extending to the center of the trunk. These samples expose a full

Large oak, growing near San Andreas fault, shows pronounced tilt caused by effects of San Francisco's 1906 earthquake.

sequence of rings, yet leave only a narrow hole that can later be plugged without doing any damage to the tree.

    Historians of earthquakes also look for old written accounts of tremors. One of the earliest quakes in North America for which there are eyewitness reports occurred in New England in the year 1638, rattling the God-fearing members of the young Massachusetts Bay Colony only 18 years after the Pilgrims landed. Contemporary accounts say that the shock was strong enough to knock over chimneys and do other minor damage. One can only wonder what sinful behavior the colony's pious elders thought might have provoked such a heavenly outburst. Still another early quake rocked the French settlements in the Quebec area, along the Saint Lawrence River, on February 5, 1663.

In California, although the earth and trees contain clues to many earlier quakes, written records go back only to 1800. They were kept by the Franciscan fathers, who unwittingly set up their missions almost parallel to California's San Andreas fault along the old Spanish highway known as the *Camino Real* ("Royal Road"). In the year 1800, long before the United States wrested California from Mexico, a rash of tremors damaged the Mission San Juan Battista, near present-day Hollister. In 1812, while the eastern part of the continent was shaking under the boots of invading British soldiers, the ground in California rumbled so often from natural causes that the Franciscan fathers spoke of it as the year of the earthquakes.

But historical records do not always give a clear-cut view of the past. While studying old documents in hopes of establishing a chronology of California earthquakes, George Louderback, a geologist at the University of California at Berkeley, learned that 40 Indians were killed by a quake on December 8, 1812, while worshipping at San Juan Capistrano, the mission famed for the annual return of its swallows. But the day of the quake happened to be a Tuesday, not a Sunday. Louderback wondered why the Indians would be attending mass on a weekday. Further inquiry revealed that the day was in fact a holy day. But that did not end the matter. Old records showed that at the time the holy day was no longer being celebrated by the Roman Catholic

Church. Could the California padres have been so out of touch with Rome that they worshipped on days of their own choosing? Louderback never found the answer. As one of his Berkeley colleagues, seismologist Bruce A. Bolt, notes, sometimes even the most diligent inquiries into the history of old quakes can bring only new complications.

There is no uncertainty about a period of extraordinary seismicity that affected an entirely different part of the country at about the same time. The quakes struck in the very heart of the continent near the little settlement of New Madrid (pronounced MAD-rid), Missouri, located along a bend of the winding Mississippi River in what was then the Louisiana Territory. The first shock came shortly before two o'clock in the morning of December 16, 1811, abruptly awakening the town's sleeping citizens with the loud creaks and groans of the shaking timbers in their houses.

The vibrations quickly worsened. Furniture overturned, crockery crashed from shelves, and brick chimneys fell. The panicked residents fled outdoors and waited anxiously in the chilly darkness for the earth to end its rage. But the worst was yet to come.

At daybreak a new round of shaking began. The upheavals continued intermittently for the next two days. Still more large shocks occurred on January 23, 1812, and again on February 7. The tremors become known collectively as the great New Madrid earthquake, as terrible a natural calamity as had yet befallen the young nation. One eyewitness wrote that "the whole land was moved and waved like waves of the sea." Another recalled that it trembled "like the flesh of a beef just killed."

As the earth did its frenzied dance, trees swayed so wildly that their tops brushed together in brief embraces. Fissures creased the ground, snapping open and closed like the jaws of an angry alligator. The skies were lit up by bolts of lightning, and thunderclaps echoed across the countryside. Sulfurous fumes, escaping from the earth, spread a foul-smelling odor of brimstone that must have seemed like a preview of hell.

The usually calm Mississippi River went wild. Turning into whirlpools and rapids, it overflowed its banks and, by some accounts, briefly reversed its course. The rampaging waters swept onto hillsides, knocked down forests, and carried boats miles inland. The ground collapsed in many places, permanently resculpturing the landscape. The bottom literally fell out of tiny Reelfoot Lake in northwestern Tennessee. What was once no more than a little swimming hole was changed by subsidence into a ten-mile-long body of water that has become a favorite of local fishermen.

The tremors were among the most powerful ever to strike the continental United States in modern history. No instruments existed at the time to record the upheavals, but the detailed reports of damage indicate that the quakes would have registered between magnitude 7 and 7.5 on the Richter scale, today's standard method for classifying quakes.

A word is in order about this famous measure, which is used by seismologists everywhere and is usually one of the first facts given in news reports about quakes. It was developed in the 1930s by the Caltech seismologist Charles F. Richter, in conjunction with Beno Gutenberg (see Chapter 6), to provide a way of comparing the strength of quakes, just as astronomers compared the magnitude, or brightness, of stars. In the Richter scale, the term magnitude means the size, or strength, of an earthquake's waves. A magnitude 3 quake is usually barely felt, magnitude 5 causes minor damage, 6 or higher may lead to widespread destruction. But the scale can be deceptive because it is logarithmic. That is, each whole number represents a tenfold increase in wave size over the previous number. Thus the waves of a magnitude 7 quake are ten times as large as those of a magnitude 6 quake, 100 times as large as those of a magnitude 5.

The scale can also be used to calculate the total amount of energy released by earthquakes. This goes up even faster. A magnitude 7 quake indicates a release of energy about 30 times as great as a magnitude 6 quake and about 1,000 times that of a magnitude 5. Scientists are constantly trying to refine the scale. After a recent study, the previously accepted value for the 1906

Seismologist Charles F. Richter, along with the instruments of his profession, at California Institute of Technology.

San Francisco quake was lowered from 8.3 to 7.9 and the Alaska's 1964 Good Friday event was raised from 8.4 to 9.2. The biggest revision involved Chile's 1960 quake. The largest quake to hit the Americas in at least a century, it had originally been rated at 8.5. Now scientists put its magnitude at 9.5, which seems to be about as powerful as a tremor can get.

Even when measured against such major quakes, the New Madrid shocks were formidable. Their circle of destruction, covering at least 50,000 square miles, spread over parts of Missouri, Arkansas, Tennessee, and Kentucky. Lesser effects were felt as far away as Canada and the east coast of the United States. Church bells started ringing in Charleston, South Carolina, pendulum clocks stopped in Washington, D.C., and windows rattled in New York City. No more than about 3,000 people lived around New Madrid at the time. The sparse level of settlement undoubtedly kept down the loss of life and property damage. Only half a dozen people are definitely known to have been killed, although as many as 100 deaths may have gone unrecorded, mostly of travelers caught by the quake-tossed waters of the Mississippi. To this day, farming in the region suffers from the sandy soil spewed out of the earth in those terrifying months.

Geologically, what is so remarkable and puzzling about the great New Madrid earthquake is that it occurred far from those seismically active zones where earthquakes are usually expected. One such region is California, bisected as it is by that famed break in its geological structure, the San Andreas fault. Even within historical times, movements along the fault have been the cause of innumerable earthquakes, large and small. But geologists, who are always on the lookout for breaks in the earth's bedrock, knew of no such flaws in the American heartland around New Madrid. They wondered why this region should have been devastated by the quakes of 1811–1812 and by numerous smaller tremors since then.

To solve the mystery, scientists of the U.S. Geological Survey, under a new federal program aimed at reducing earthquake risks, began examining the subterranean structure of the Mississippi River Valley in the late 1970s. For their investigation, they turned to a technique called seismic profiling, a nondestructive form of exploration long used in the search for oil. In effect, it involves the artificial creation of tiny earthquakes for use as geological probes. As the man-made seismic waves travel through the ground, their speed varies, depending on the rock's density, rigidity, and ability to resist compression. By carefully clocking the echoes of these waves as they bounce off different layers of rock, or strata, scientists can develop a precise profile, or map, of the underground formations.

Such helpful miniquakes can be triggered by various methods. In remote regions, seismologists often detonate small explosive charges or release bursts of compressed air. But in this case, since they were working in a populated area, they employed a less noisy method of ground-shaking developed by the oil industry. It involved the use of large trucks equipped with powerful vibrating pads that resemble the mechanical feet of a giant robot out of a science-fiction film. Lowered from the undersides of the vehicles, the pads shook the ground, sending off waves in every direction. As they reflected off different layers of rock, the echoes were picked up by special receivers called geophones, which had been scattered over the area under study, and piped into computers. Rapidly analyzing the flood of incoming data, the high-speed electronic whizzes turned the signals into exact charts of the Mississippi Valley's hitherto unknown subterranean geology.

These geophysical maps confirmed dramatically what the scientists had suspected all along. The underground layers of rock were riddled with cracks, places where the strata were interrupted and offset vertically. Some of the breaks looked like steps. At one time in the earth's remote past, the different layers had followed smooth parallel paths that were more or less straight and unbroken. Now, the seismic profiles showed, they were broken and displaced. Along some segments, the layers had dropped as much as 3,000 feet below their original positions. The scientists could only speculate about what wrought this subterranean havoc. Plainly, an incredibly powerful force was at work, tearing apart and shifting tons upon tons of rock.

The scientists had discovered a zone of major faults, great rips in the fabric of the earth. These had remained totally hidden from the prying eyes of geologists under a thick covering of muddy sediments deposited over the ages by the Mississippi River. The U.S. Geological Survey had mapped only Arkansas's Mississippi and Craighead counties, but the newly found zone turned out to be just one small section of a larger fault system uncovered by other investigators. Since 1974, scientists at Saint Louis University have been monitoring quakes in the central part of the Mississippi Valley with a network of seismographs spread over five states. By noting every occurrence of a quake with a dot on a map, they found that the markings indicated a fault zone at least 75 miles long, zigzagging from Arkansas through Missouri and into southern Illinois.

The original movements that created these faults probably took place about 300 million years ago, long before the age of the dinosaurs. But even today, as Saint Louis University's seismic data shows, the earth under the Mississippi Valley has not stopped shifting. One telltale sign is the matching, if much smaller, displacements that have occurred in more recent times in the shallow—and thus much younger—sediments near the surface. There is also more visible evidence of earth movement: the thousands of minor quakes that have shaken the Mississippi River Valley since the three big jolts of 1811–1812.

The vast majority of these temblors are much too weak to jar anything more than Saint Louis University's seismographic network. But they are a worrisome hint of future disasters; they show that the same mighty forces that first ripped the rock apart are still far from tamed. Indeed, one of the most intriguing findings in the flurry of discoveries about America's shaky heartland is that the fault zone lies in the very middle of what appears to be a much more awesome geological phenomenon: a very ancient rift, or thinning, in the earth's crust. The evidence, still tentative as yet, suggests that about half a billion years ago the entire continent slowly and inexplicably started to break apart. Then, just as mysteriously, it stopped its movement before there was a major separation. Only the buried scars of that break in the crust remain as a reminder of these primordial events.

The new findings are more than simply a triumph of the latest techniques of geophysical exploration. After patiently studying the Mississippi Valley's seismic activity, researchers have finally been able to link its quakes with actual physical structures in the earth. This new understanding of the area's chaotic geology should have important practical value. Just as meteorologists use cloud formations and other atmospheric conditions to forecast storms, so seismologists are looking to the faults as seismic warning signs. By keeping track of the movements along them, they hope to see whether dangerous stresses are building up that will result in new quakes. Eventually they may even be able to tell when and where the next big quake will strike. In today's highly populated Mississippi Valley, such a prediction could save countless lives.

As for the current residents of New Madrid (population: about 3,000), they seem to be taking the threat of another big jolt in stride. "All of us who grew up around here have felt earthquakes," the part-time mayor, Jimmy Cravens, told a reporter a few years ago. "It makes good coffee-shop conversation. That's about all." It also helps commerce, apparently. In his antique shop, a popular item he had on sale was a T-shirt imprinted with the words VISIT NEW MADRID (WHILE IT'S STILL THERE).

4 AN EARTHQUAKE PRIMER

The simplest way to describe an earthquake is as a shaking of the ground. Yet that dictionary definition does not really say much about quakes. Nor would it seem very satisfying to anyone who has had to endure their violent, nerve-wracking motions. The important question is, what causes the shaking in the first place? The answer is not so simple.

The fact is that the ground almost always shakes—from the pounding of wind and ocean waves, from the vibrations of passing vehicles, even from the daily expansion and contraction of the outer few inches of the earth's crust caused by solar heating. Scientists have a name for these tiny earth movements: microseisms, from the Greek words for "small" and "shaking." But this seismic background "noise" is so weak that only the most sensitive instruments can detect it. Human activity sometimes causes larger quakes. The detonation of explosives, both chemical and nuclear, can tremble the ground and, as noted in Chapter 3, help earth scientists understand its hidden structure. So can the collapse of a mine shaft or cave, the rush of moving earth in a landslide or avalanche, and the impact of a meteorite. Earthquakes often precede or accompany volcanic eruptions, which are triggered by the pressure of hot gases and molten rock called magma trying to escape from deep within the earth. (At least in this case, Aristotle was partly right in attributing quakes to fiery underground vapors.)

But the quakes that do the most damage—those blockbusters that can destroy cities—are caused by something quite different: the gradual accumulation of strain, or deforming forces, in the earth's bedrock. Though rock may seem hard, it has natural elasticity. Under continuous pressure, it will gradually bend, stretch, or compress, all the while storing the energy exerted on it, like a clock spring that is slowly being wound. There are nonetheless limits to the rock's elasticity and energy-storage capacity. If the pressure keeps building up, these limits will be exceeded with catastrophic results. Suddenly, the rock will snap, releasing its energy in a flurry of furious vibrations, almost as if it were a giant bell struck by a clapper. The vibrations will radiate outward in all directions, violently shaking the ground as they course through it.

Seismic vibrations take the form of characteristic waves, which carry the quake's energy from one place to another. Like all waves, they come in many different types and strengths. Some travel by alternately compressing and expanding the ground in their path, just as sound waves move by pushing, then pulling, the air. Others ripple the ground from side to side, like the undulations in a snapping whip. Still others move up and down, like the quivers in a bowl of pudding. Two like waves may come together and amplify each other. Passing from one material to another, they may be refracted, or bent, or sometimes stopped altogether. If there is one generalization that can be made about earthquake waves, it is that they are extremely complicated (more will be said about them in Chapter 6).

An Earthquake Primer

The waves are produced by fractures of the earth's crust. They usually occur along pre-existing cracks in the ground known as faults. These are lines of weakness where the rock may have been severed by previous quakes. If the fracturing spreads over a large section of the fault, great masses of rock will be jarred and the ground will convulse over a huge area, sometimes hundreds of miles from the original break.

The man who first helped explain how rock could behave in this strange way was a geology professor at Johns Hopkins University, in Baltimore, named Harry Fielding Reid. After the great 1906 San Francisco earthquake, Reid went west to begin a detailed study of what had happened. He quickly realized that there had been spectacular ground movements along great stretches of the San Andreas fault. Land on one side of this geological divide had slipped sharply past that on the other. Such shifts were especially noticeable wherever highways crossed the fault. At these junctures, the roadways had literally been ripped apart. The paving had been pushed aside, or offset, by as much as 21 feet. But Reid's geological sleuthing also uncovered some totally unexpected movements.

Examining old surveying markers along the fault, he found that significant ground shifts had taken place long before the quake. In the preceding half-century, signs once facing each other directly across the fault had slipped sideways from one another by as much as 12 feet. What distinguished these earlier movements from those that occurred during the quake was that they were extremely slow. The ground crept along only a few inches a year.

To earth scientists of the time, movements of earth in advance of a quake were a thoroughly mystifying phenomenon. But Reid was a shrewd scientific detective. In the years before the calam-

Aerial view of California's great seismic divide, the San Andreas fault, a boundary between two tectonic plates.

ity, he realized, horizontal forces had been quietly exerting pressure in opposing directions along the fault. Slowly and inexorably, the rock was being squeezed and stretched. It appeared to be in the steely grip of powerful underground forces. On one side of the fault, these forces seemed to be pulling the rock in a generally northerly direction; on the other, to the south. As time passed, the strain on the rock increased. When the material could store no more energy—when its elasticity was stretched to the limit—it broke. The results were jolting, to say the least. Almost instantly, billions of tons of bedrock lurched apart, the severed halves tearing away from each other along many miles of fault. With an incredible burst of noise, heat, and shaking, the earth had finally released its pent-up energy.

Reid's novel insight was this: while earthquakes may seem to strike unannounced, they actually give plenty of forewarning with the gradual build-up of stresses in the rock. As he explained in his report on the San Francisco quake: "It is impossible for rock to rupture without first being subjected to elastic strains greater than it can endure." As for the quake itself, it was simply the tumultuous finale of a drama long in the making: the moment when the overstressed rock, like the overwound spring, snapped back to a relaxed position. Since Reid proposed his "elastic rebound" theory, it has been verified repeatedly. Slow ground movements seem to have preceded virtually every major quake ever studied.

By clarifying what happens to rock before and during tremors, Reid's work added significantly to the theoretical understanding of earthquakes. It also had an important side effect. For the first time in the history of seismology, scientists had found a possible method of predicting earthquakes. Reid showed that significant ground movements preceded quakes. In effect, these movements were warnings—or, as scientists say,

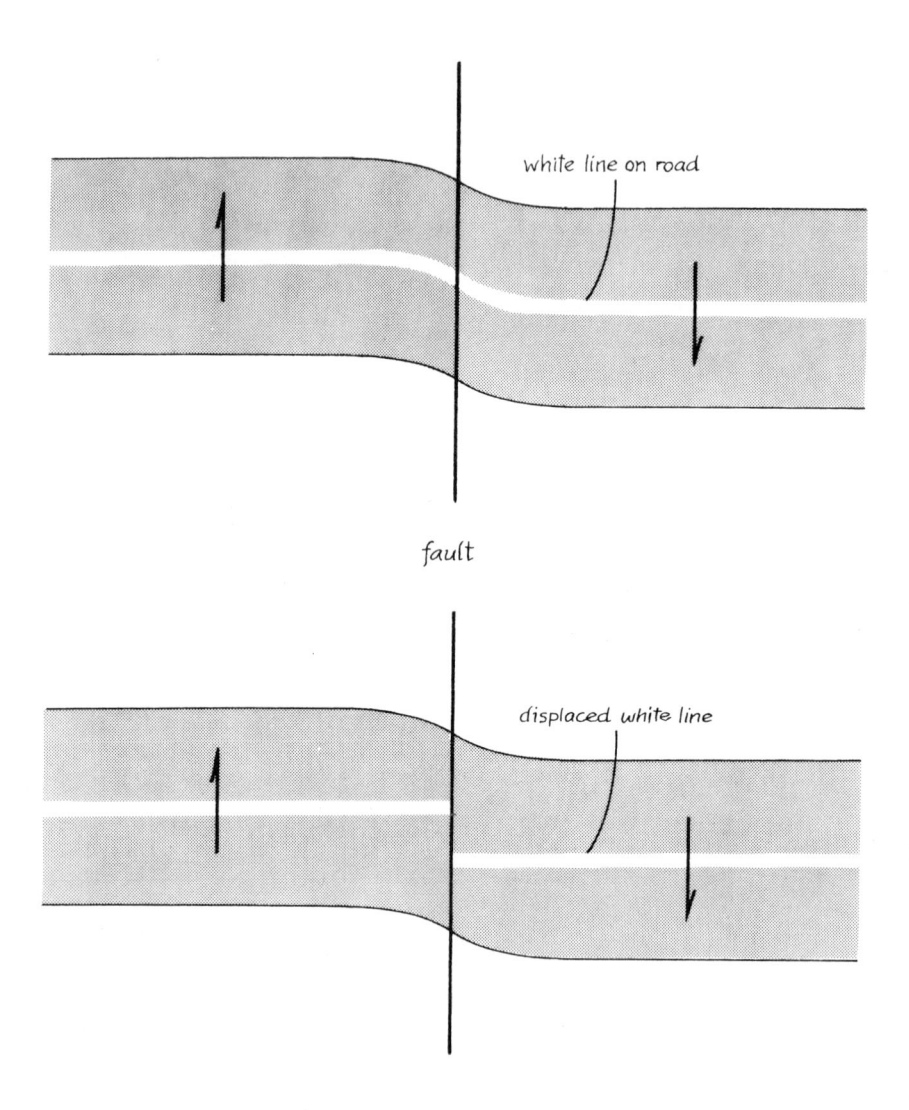

Diagrams show elastic rebound theory at work. In top drawing, strain builds in opposing directions along roadway crossing fault and bends rock on either side. In lower drawing, rock has snapped to a relaxed position after reaching breaking point, leaving road noticeably offset.

An Earthquake Primer

precursors—of an imminent quake. Just how imminent could perhaps be determined in the future by measuring how much movement had already occurred along an active fault. Then it would be only a simple matter of subtracting that number from the total movement that had occurred before the last quake. In this way, a would-be forecaster might be able to figure out how much additional movement would have to take place before the earth ruptured again.

In the case of the San Francisco area, Reid already knew the amount of prequake motion along the San Andreas fault. He also knew the average annual rate of movement. So it was easy for him to estimate how much time would probably have to elapse before another quake. He predicted that the San Francisco section of the San Andreas fault would not be jolted by a major upheaval for another century.

Reid's forecasting method was not very exact. It also was based on an unproved assumption that the elasticity of rock remains the same after a quake as it was before. Nor was it very practical. In Reid's day, no instruments existed to monitor the slow, inching movements along a fault with anything like the precision needed to make reasonably accurate predictions. Still, by suggesting the possibility of forecasting quakes in a scientific way, Reid had taken a major step forward. Eventually, other scientists would begin to turn the dream implicit in his work into reality.

Invaluable as the elastic rebound theory was, it left unanswered certain questions. What makes the rock move in the first place? And where do these powerful earth-moving forces originate? One clue lies in the rugged face of the planet itself. Everywhere geologists turn they find evidence that the earth has been shaped and reshaped in countless ways. Mountains rise out of the earth's crust. Layers of rock, piled atop one another like crumpled carpets, twist and bend in every direction. Such great faults as the San Andreas slash crazily across the landscape. These observations point to an unavoidable conclusion: as solid and immovable as the earth's crust may look, it is in fact being pushed and pummeled by forces powerful enough to destroy it.

In the nineteenth century, many scientists were convinced that the explanation for all these movements could be found in the gradual cooling and contraction of the earth. They believed that the planet began its life as a hot, fiery ball, not unlike the sun itself. Then it slowly started to shed its heat into space, venting the fiery gases in its interior through volcanoes. As it began to shrink from the loss of the gases, its crust shriveled, like the skin of a dried-up apple, only on a far grander scale. In some places, the contractions created mountains and valleys. In others, they stretched the land into sprawling plateaus. Still elsewhere, they left behind the great ocean basins. And the contractions, the scientists said, were continuing, occasionally rippling the earth's crust with violent tremors. So went the explanation for earthquakes.

The theory seemed persuasive enough, at least for a while. No wonder: it had been proposed by no less an authority than Isaac Newton, discoverer of the laws of gravitation and motion. In 1681 he spoke of "ye breaking out of vapours from below before the earth was well hardened, the settling & shrinking of ye whole globe after ye upper regions or surface began to be hard." But by the end of the nineteenth century, difficulties had arisen. As geologists inspected the earth's mountain ranges, they realized that their size and shape would have required far more contracting than could be explained by a slowly cooling earth. Still another problem came with the discovery of radioactivity, a process by which elements like radium and uranium give off energy, partly in the form of heat, when the nuclei of their atoms spontaneously split. If materials within the earth were producing heat, could the planet be cooling off? More likely its temperature would be rising. Skeptical scientists raised another objection. If mountains were really formed by a cooling earth, why were they not spread evenly all over the globe, like the wrinkles on the apple, rather than limited to certain ranges?

As scientists pondered these questions, they realized that they had to look for other explanations of the forces at work within the earth. Some suggested that the earth was in fact expanding because of a weakening of gravity, the "glue" holding it together. But eventually this and other ideas fell before an all-encompassing theory called plate tectonics. (From the Greek word for "builder," tectonics is the geological term for the creation of structures in the earth's crust, especially by folding and faulting.) Now generally accepted by earth scientists, plate tectonics provides a unifying explanation for all major earthly phenomena, everything from mountain building to the slow drift of continents, from the formation of volcanoes to the occurrence of earthquakes. But the emergence of this startling—indeed, revolutionary—world view pushes us a little ahead of the story, so we leave the unfolding of plate tectonics to later chapters. Meanwhile, there is more to say about the actual mechanism of quakes; what really happens when the earth quivers and shakes.

To learn more about any scientific subject, investigators must collect data, usually by making measurements. Only through painstaking examination of detail does the whole picture begin to emerge. The study of earthquakes is no exception. One of the first things that scientists do is to determine just how strong a particular quake may have been. In this way, one quake can be compared with another. But how to rate a phenomenon as powerful as an earthquake, which can unleash more energy than dozens of hydrogen bombs? The simplest solution might be a scale based on the damage that earthquakes do and on the impressions of the people who lived through it. The number 1 could represent a quake that barely shakes the ground; 2 a quake that tumbles dishes from shelves and pictures off walls; 3 a quake that cracks plaster and knocks down chimneys; and so on.

The very first extensive scientific investigation of an earthquake involved the creation of just such a measuring tool. In December 1857 the southern part of Italy was hit by a devastating quake. When Robert Mallet, an Irish engineer, learned of the disaster, he immediately applied for travel funds from the Royal Society in London and headed for the kingdom of Naples to survey the damage.

At first glance, the undertaking seemed a curious one for someone like Mallet. He came from a country where earthquakes are relatively rare. He was also occupied with managing his family's highly successful foundry and engineering works. Under his astute guidance, it had built railroad stations and central heating systems throughout the British Isles, spanned Ireland's River Shannon with swivel bridges, cast mortars and cannon for the British army and navy, and rebuilt the famed Fastnet Rock Lighthouse off Ireland's southernmost point. But Mallet had another passion. Ever since reading a book about them as a young man, he had yearned to learn more about earthquakes. Now he finally had the chance to study the effects of a major quake firsthand.

Notebook in hand and guided by a compass and measuring stick, he spent two months combing the battered countryside east of Naples. The area was in shambles. More than 10,000 people had been killed. Two villages were totally destroyed, others were heavily damaged. As he later recalled:

An Earthquake Primer

When the observer first enters upon one of those earthquake-shaken towns, he finds himself in the midst of utter confusion. The eye is bewildered by "a city become a heap." He wanders over masses of dislocated stone and mortar. Houses seem to have been precipitated to the ground in every direction.... There seems no governing law, nor any indication of a prevailing direction of [the] overturning force.

Working his way thorugh the chaos, Mallet let nothing escape his sharp eye. He observed such details as the direction of cracks in walls and the way columns, bricks, and tombstones had fallen. He even got dazed residents to recollect what the earth's movements felt like at the very moment of the shocks. To organize this mountain of data, he did what any good engineer would do. He devised a way of classifying the damage by creating a scale. Mallet's scale rated the damage at each site, or what modern scientists call the earthquake's intensity. He was not the first person to suggest an earthquake intensity scale.° The pioneer was a physician named Domenico Pignataro, who lived in the same quake-prone part of Italy during the late eighteenth century. Based on personal reports of casualties and damage that were made to him, he began rating quakes as either slight, moderate, strong, or very strong. But Mallet had a leg up on his predecessor, so to speak. By walking through the battered area himself,

---

°Nor was Mallet the last. Today the internationally accepted scale for describing the intensity of quakes is one based on the work of another pioneering seismologist, the Italian priest Giuseppi Mercalli (1850–1914). Called the Modified Mercalli Scale, it has 12 intensities, designated by Roman numerals. They range from I (the quake is barely felt by people at the site), through VI (plaster walls crack, tables slide, chimneys are damaged, and many people run outdoors), to XII (the ground tosses visibly up and down, objects fly wildly into the air, and all structures collapse). Unlike magnitude, which is an absolute measure of an earthquake's strength at its place of origin, intensity varies from area to area. Thus, while a quake has only one magnitude, it usually has many intensities.

he eliminated the inconsistencies that would have been introduced by using different observers.

In his first category, Mallet placed towns that had suffered the most damage and the greatest number of casualties; in the second, those that had lost only their largest buildings and some lives; in the third, communities where damage was minor and there were no deaths; and in the fourth, villages where the people felt shaking but sustained no real damage. Transferring his findings to a map of the region, he designated each area according to his scale. Then he connected places of equal damage with lines that he called isoseismals (from the Greek words for "equal shaking"), a name that has stuck ever since.

Mallet's systematic approach quickly paid off. His isoseismals formed roughly into a series of overlapping circles, one nestling within another, with the innermost enclosing the area of severest damage. Thus Mallet managed to locate the heart of the shaking, the quake's epicenter. His carefully plotted map also told him how the intensity of the quake had diminished over distance. That gave him a rough indication of its size. Then he turned to the telltale cracks and fallen pillars. Using them as pointers, he determined the direction of the earthquake waves and the approximate angle at which they emerged from the ground. Taking such "sightings" from several different observation points, an exercise in geometry called triangulation, he found where in the ground the wave pathways met. This was the place, Mallet proclaimed, where the shaking began: the site of the actual break in the earth's bedrock, or the quake's focus. It was located seven miles into the earth directly below the epicenter.

Mallet's investigations extended beyond Italy. Back at home, he had already measured how fast the waves travel through the ground. Since Ireland rarely has quakes, he created his own—

An Earthquake Primer

by exploding gunpowder in different types of soil. Peering through a telescope, he clocked how much time elapsed before he could see mercury quivering in bowls that he had set up at known distances from the explosions. From these experiments, he calculated that seismic waves traveled about twice as fast (at about 1,100 miles per hour) through hard rock as through loose, sandy soil. Mallet also scoured Europe's libraries for every piece of writing he could find on earthquakes dating back to ancient times. Eventually he produced references for nearly 7,000 quakes. These enabled him to draw a trailblazing seismic map of the world, showing where quakes had been reported as far back as 1606 B.C. The chart indicated more vividly and dramatically than ever before that earthquakes occurred much more frequently in some parts of the world than in others. One such area was the so-called Ring of Fire, a region of frequent quakes and recurrent volcanic eruptions rimming the Pacific Ocean all the way from California to Japan and from Alaska to the South Seas. Neither Mallet nor his contemporaries could explain the ring. But just viewing earthquake patterns in this global way helped point scientific thinking in the right direction.

In 1862 Mallet published two beautifully illustrated volumes called *The Great Neapolitan Earthquake of 1857: The First Principles of Observational Seismology*, which became a classic of its kind. Besides giving birth to the word "seismology" for the scientific study of quakes, it concluded correctly that an earthquake is caused "by the sudden flexure and constraint of the elastic materials forming a portion of the earth's crust, or by their giving way and becoming fractured." For nearly half a century, until Reid's exhaustive investigation of the San Francisco disaster, Mallet's work reigned as the definitive study of an individual earthquake.

Yet before the new science of seismology could make further strides, it needed more sophisticated tools and techniques. Mallet had used his measuring sticks and bowls of mercury to study seismic waves. But these gave him only the roughest kind of measurements. His damage scale also had serious limitations. A tumbled building might reflect more on the structure's poor design than on a quake's true power. In unpopulated areas, where there are no buildings to knock down, the scale would have been useless. Clearly, seismology required an instrument that could measure the strength of any quake, regardless of where it struck. Such devices were slow in coming. There was, of course, Chang Heng's elaborate dragon pot (see Chapter 3), but knowledge of this clever gadget was lost until modern times. By the 1700s, Europeans began using artfully balanced objects or bowls filled with water, mercury, and other liquids that would respond to tremors. But such detectors, or seismoscopes, were of limited value. They could only pick up the shaking without providing any measurements. Sometimes the gadgets' movements were so slight they could barely be seen at all.

The first crude instruments that could actually measure the strength of quakes appeared in the middle of the eighteenth century. These early seismometers relied on a pendulumlike weight, usually a bob of lead, suspended by a wire from the ceiling. When a quake shook the building, the weight remained momentarily stationary, even while the floor below it moved. To take advantage of the bob's laggardness—a resistance to motion that physicists call inertia—scientists would attach a marker to the bottom of the weight. As the earth moved beneath the bob, the marker would leave a tracing on some surface. One version of such a seismometer appeared in Italy in 1751. The free-swinging mass was set up so that it could make scratches in a smooth layer of sand on a tray. From the length of the grooves carved into the sand during an earthquake, scientists could judge roughly how powerful the jolt had been.

The first of these pendulum-type instruments recorded only quake motions that were to and fro, or horizontal. But as seismometers became more sophisticated in the nineteenth century, some were devised to register the ground's vertical movements. The weight in these devices was held either by a pivoting arm

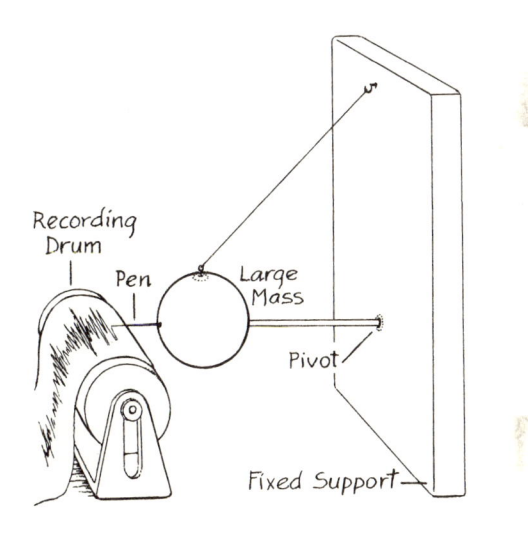

Simplified view of seismograph. During quake, heavy weight attached to pivoting arm lags behind other parts of instrument as it is being shaken. This allows pen on weight to sketch wavy lines on rotating drum that represent the quake's waves. In this arrangement, the seismograph records sideways, or horizontal, motion of the ground. To record vertical movements, the weight would have to be suspended from overhead so it could move up and down.

attached to a side wall or by a spring, enabling it to swing up and down rather than back and forth. Another improvement was the addition of a slowly revolving drum of paper and the attachment of a pen to the weight. As the drum slowly turned, the pen left a tracing of the earth's vibrations on it. These markings are called a seismogram. During periods of seismic calm, the markings would be relatively smooth, except for an occasional squiggle caused by the footsteps of passersby or the rumble of vehicles. But when the ground came alive during a quake, the pen would go into a frenzy, leaving a wild, zigzagging pattern. Each of the pen's swings represented the arrival of another earthquake wave—the bigger the swing, the more powerful the wave. Leaving a permanent record of a quake's vibrations, the instrument was a true seismograph. At last earthquake researchers had the basic tool they needed to study the earth's spasms.

No one did more to perfect the new device than the adventurous English geologist John Milne. Born in Liverpool in 1850, he had tramped across Ireland as a youth, paying for his room and board by playing the piano in roadside inns. Later he canoed the rivers and canals of southern England. At age 21, he and a companion explored a glacier in Iceland. After finishing his studies as a mining engineer at King's College in London, he prospected for minerals in Newfoundland and the rugged wastes of the Sinai desert. In 1875 he was one of a number of British scientists invited to join the faculty of the new Imperial College of Engineering in Tokyo. It was a time of tremendous ferment and change for Japan. Not too many years earlier Japan's long isolation had been ended by a U.S. naval expedition under Commodore Matthew Perry. And the engineering school had been set up as part of Japan's effort to master Western science and technology. The Japanese had a quaint term for their academic guests from the West: "honorable foreign menial."

An Earthquake Primer

In characteristic fashion, the young professor of geology and mining took the most daring route to his new assignment. Instead of traveling by ship, Milne went overland by coach and sled via Russia and Siberia, a difficult, wintry journey that lasted seven months. On his first night in Tokyo early in 1876, he was welcomed by a small earthquake. Later Milne would recall, "We had earthquakes for breakfast, dinner, supper and to sleep on." Initially he concentrated on teaching, acquainting himself with his new country and studying its geology, particularly Japan's volcanoes. Waving off the warnings of friends, he scaled the seething mountains to see firsthand the activity in their bubbling vents.

But in 1880 Tokyo's neighboring city of Yokohama was partially destroyed by a severe quake. Striking so close to home, the event was one he could not ignore. From then on, Milne threw himself totally into the task of trying to understand this deadly phenomenon. Recognizing that he would need the help of many people to study earthquakes, he called a meeting of Japanese and foreign scientists and formed the Seismological Society of Japan. To gather data, he devised a beautifully simple scheme that appealed to the methodical Japanese. Each week Milne sent off batches of self-addressed postcards to officials in every large town within 100 miles of Tokyo. They were asked to answer specific questions about any tremors that might have been felt in their areas during the previous seven days. The Japanese bureaucrats responded with a flood of weekly information from which Milne made detailed charts and maps marking the location, strength, and range of every recorded jolt.

Yet Milne recognized a weakness in his study. As thorough as his Japanese correspondents were, he knew that any conclusions based on the impressions of a wide variety of untrained observers could not be very precise. To obtain accurate and consistent information, he needed scientific instruments that could accurately detect, measure, and record seismic waves. Some devices were already available at the Imperial College, but they were neither reliable nor exact. With the help of two British colleagues, James Alfred Ewing and Thomas Gray, he began designing his own seismograph. For many weeks the college's technical staff worked into the night putting together various trial models. Milne did not wait for natural quakes to test his handiwork. He boldly created his own by dropping heavy weights or detonating explosives. At least once his enthusiasm backfired when, as he reported with self-mocking humor, a blast lifted "about a ton of earth, flattening me and the instrument alike, and bringing that experiment to an untimely end."

But the risks were not taken for naught. After a year of experimenting, Milne and his colleagues produced a seismograph that was a scientific breakthrough. Elegantly simple in design, it could record tremors so faint they were all but undetectable by other instruments. It could also be set up to respond to any of the ground's motions during a quake—up and down, side to side, or to and fro. To capture all three movements simultaneously, Milne would arrange three instruments in a row, each at a different angle but with their recording drums rotating at the same rate. While pens traced out the vibrations on rolls of paper, spring motors drove the drums for as long as 24 hours.

A perfectionist always, Milne never stopped trying to make improvements. To eliminate the friction between the pen and paper, which distorted the shape of the tracings, he substituted light beams and photographic paper. To keep the pendulum from swinging excessively and amplifying the readings, he devised mechanisms that damped any extra motion. To tell exactly when the first waves arrived, he installed clocks in his seismographs. So effective were the new instruments that they soon became the standard at seismological stations everywhere.

Milne was a methodical observer. He noticed that his seismographs would vibrate mysteriously at times when no quake had been reported in the vicinity. He wondered what was shaking the instruments. Scouring the earthquake records of seismic stations on the Asian mainland and even farther away, he found the answer: the seismograms from the distant observatories contained tracings that were exact duplicates of his own puzzling observations. His instruments, performing even better than he expected, had managed to detect quakes that occurred hundreds of miles away.

More of an experimenter than a theorist, Milne preferred to leave speculations about earthquakes to others. Indeed, it was a Japanese geologist, Bunjiro Koto, not Milne, who concluded correctly after one major quake in Japan that it is the movement of faults that causes earthquakes, rather than vice versa. Koto's observation was an important theoretical advance in grasping the mechanism of quakes. Until then, the commonly accepted view of scientists was just the opposite: that it is earthquakes that create faults. Nevertheless, Milne also made important contributions to understanding quakes. He discovered, for example, that seismic waves do not all have the same velocity, even when they are traveling in the same material. Studying his seismograms, he found that the first waves to arrive were invariably those he called "condensational" waves, or a back-and-forth movement of the ground. They were followed by larger "distortional" waves, which shake the ground up and down and from side to side. Clearly, the condensational waves were the faster of the two, a relationship that he astutely realized could be used as a yardstick to determine how far off a quake had occurred.

If a quake struck relatively close by, the two types of waves arrived in rapid succession. If it occurred at a great distance, there would be a considerable interval between their arrivals. Milne worked out a precise ratio between time and distance. If, say, the waves came 90 seconds apart—something he could readily tell from his seismographs' built-in clocks—it turned out that the quake's epicenter was some 450 miles away. An interval of two minutes meant a distance of 600 miles; two and a half minutes, 700 miles; and so forth. With this work Milne also showed that it was possible to pinpoint the epicenter of a far-off quake. All it took were simultaneous readings from three seismic stations located some distance apart and some simple geometry. On a map the seismologist would draw a circle centered on each observatory. The radii of these circles would be determined by the varying arrival times of the waves at the different stations. Where the three circles intersected lay the quake's epicenter.

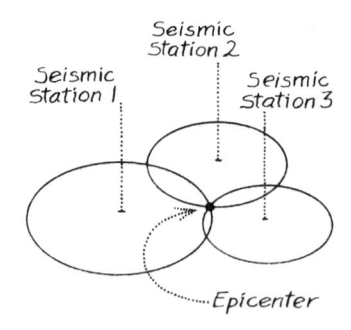

Earthquake is located by reckoning its distance from three seismic stations, then drawing circles centered on these listening posts using the measurements as the radii. Epicenter lies at meeting place of the three circles.

Milne was so diligent a collector of earthquake data that a Japanese colleague once complained that "he threatens to exhaust all that there is for workers in seismology to investigate." Milne accounted for no less than two-thirds of the Seismological Society's published material. He left few questions about quakes untouched; he even considered whether animals could sense them ahead of time. He concluded that while animals might feel tremors somewhat before humans, they probably could not be used for early warnings. Milne also wrote three textbooks, as well as a graphically illustrated volume on the 1891 quake that devastated the agricultural Neo Valley west of Tokyo, killing nearly 10,000 people. Besides his scholarly work, he immersed himself totally in Japan's cultural life, studying Japanese customs, art, and religion. He became a connoisseur of sake, the national drink, and married the beautiful daughter of a Buddhist priest from the northern island of Hokkaido.

In 1895, just as he seemed ready to sign up for a third ten-year contract at the Imperial College, Milne was struck by personal disaster. A fire destroyed his home, his library, and many of his instruments. Perhaps because of this devastating loss, or perhaps because he regretted being out of the mainstream of Western science for so long, or perhaps because of alarm over the sharp upswing in Japanese nationalism, Milne decided to return home. In an extraordinary farewell tribute to a foreigner, he was received by the emperor and presented with the Order of the Rising Sun for his contributions to Japan.

Back in Europe, Milne settled with his wife on the Isle of Wight, off England's southern coast. He chose the island because it made an ideal site for a seismic observatory. Its brittle, chalky foundations vibrated readily to distant earthquakes. But seismology was now forging ahead so rapidly that even the old master could not keep up with all the varied developments. Still, his voice remained an important one. At his urging, seismological stations were established throughout the far-flung British Empire and in other nations as well, and their data were collected and analyzed by Milne. From his residence-*cum*-observatory, a pretty, tree-shaded old building called Shide Hill House, Milne regularly sent out detailed earthquake reports known as the *Shide Circulars*. These became regular reading for seismologists around the world. When Milne died in 1913, at the age of 62, seismologists everywhere mourned their loss.

5 CONTINENTS ON THE MOVE

Lying at the top of the world between Canada and northern Europe, Greenland is a bleak and forbidding place. Until modern times, it was inhabited largely by Inuits.° When the Norse chieftain Eric the Red discovered the huge island in the tenth century, he thought an inviting name might help attract settlers. Except in the south, though, there is very little green in Greenland. Even in summer, when Greenland is bathed in 24 hours of daylight, all but a narrow strip of coastal land remains covered by a thick, permanent sheet of ice. Conditions are much worse in winter. Gale winds regularly whip across the icy interior, temperatures plummet to 60 or 70 degrees below zero Fahrenheit, and life on the glaciated wasteland becomes a battle for survival.

No one understood these dangers better than a German scientist and explorer named Alfred Lothar Wegener, who had a lifelong and ultimately tragic fascination for this desolate and lonely corner of the world. He first journeyed to Greenland in 1906, as a vigorous young man in his twenties, and remained for

---

°The native peoples of the north prefer to be known by this name rather than as Eskimos, a word devised by white men from the Indian expression for "eater of raw meat."

Alfred Wegener, the great proponent of continental drift, whose radical ideas belatedly were found to be a scientific truth.

two difficult winters. In 1913, on the eve of World War I, he returned to make a daring crossing of the high-domed icecap. His only companions on that exhausting 700-mile march were a Danish colleague and a handful of ponies. The animals were used instead of dogs to haul the expedition's five sledges. Only a year before, the British explorer Robert Falcon Scott, also relying on ponies in his race with the Norwegian Roald Amundsen to the South Pole, perished together with all his men.

A generation later, in 1930, Wegener set out once more for Greenland. The journey obviously entailed risks for a man of his age. By then he was nearly 50 years old and no longer in good health. But Wegener was determined to go. Beyond the enticement of seeing Greenland again, he was driven by a desire to answer certain scientific questions. A meteorologist by profession, he wanted to study firsthand how the brutally cold, high-level streams of air sweep off the icy Greenland plateau and help shape Europe's weather. He also hoped to settle the old debate about the thickness of Greenland's icecap—whether the ice is piled up only a few hundred feet or many miles. (The answer turned out to be a little more than a mile.)

Wegener, however, had still another mission, one that he had long seemed destined to make. For nearly two decades, in lectures and writings, he had championed a bold and highly controversial theory. He was a dedicated believer in continental drift, the idea that the earth's great landmasses are slowly moving, shifting their positions in relation to one another and gradually altering the appearance of the planet. So fervently did he pursue his vision that friends and colleagues alike warned him that the obsession with drift was jeopardizing his scientific career.

Early in the century, continental drift was totally out of the mainstream of scientific opinion. Most geologists maintained that the continents were—and had always been—firmly anchored in place. Wegener challenged this orthodoxy. He and his small band of supporters insisted that the continents had wandered across the face of the earth in ages past and were continuing to move today.

Wegener's heresy was greeted with understandable disbelief by members of the scientific establishment. They could not imagine huge chunks of the earth's crust floating about like so many pieces of cracked ice in a polar sea. The theory seemed totally at odds with every accepted geophysical principle. Even Wegener acknowledged the objections to his ideas. But he also realized their possible importance if they were true. In one theoretical swoop, they could get at the root of many terrestrial mysteries: how the oceans and continents were born, what raises mountains and volcanoes, why some parts of the earth are so often wracked by quakes and others not. Continental drift was, in short, a single unifying explanation for widely differing aspects of the earth's surface.

As part of this global view, Wegener was convinced that Greenland was gradually floating westward, edging ever farther from Europe. From astronomical sightings made by previous expeditions, he estimated that it was moving at a velocity of up to 40 yards a year. Most scientists were highly skeptical of the figure; at that rate Greenland would circle the earth in less than one million years. To still the skeptics and brush away their doubts about continental drift, Wegener needed new and more convincing astronomical evidence. Consequently, one of the prime objectives of his latest journey to the Arctic was to obtain sightings that would clearly show changes in Greenland's longitude over the years.

Radical as they were, Wegener's notions about the earth were not entirely new. As early as the seventeenth century, when world maps first showed the close fit between the opposing coasts of the Americas and Africa, some people began thinking of the continents as if they were parts of what had once been a single landmass. With only a small stretch of the imagination, they could fit Brazil's equatorial bulge right under the bight of West Africa and the coast of North America snugly against North Africa, like pieces of a giant jigsaw puzzle.

Early geologists had a ready explanation for the matching coastlines. To account for the geographic curiosity, they said that the young earth had experienced a whole series of calamities that reshaped its face. Largely influenced by the Bible, this school of thought became known as catastrophism. The most frequently cited catastrophe was Noah's flood, so vividly described in the Book of Genesis as inundating the earth after 40 days and 40 nights of unending rain. In 1668 the French monk François Placet wrote that "before the Deluge, America was not separated from the other parts of the world." In 1756, as proof that the continents were broken apart by the Biblical flood, the German theologian Theodor Christoph Lilienthal cited a passage in Genesis ("The name of one was Peleg; for in his days was the earth divided"). Why else, Lilienthal wondered, would "the facing coasts of many countries, though separated by the sea, have a congruent shape . . . for example, the southern parts of America and Africa"?

Early in the nineteenth century, the German explorer and naturalist Alexander von Humboldt turned Noah's flood into a veritable global tidal wave. Sweeping across the young planet, Humboldt's torrent carved out the Atlantic basin and left behind the matching shorelines on each side of the ocean. In 1858 an American writer named Antonio Snider-Pellegrini, living in France, proposed a more catastrophic scenario. As the earth cooled and hardened, he said, most of the continental material gathered on one side of the planet. The great weight created such internal stresses that the earth's surface fractured and volcanoes erupted. At the same time, the floodwaters drenched the landscape. Only when the Americas were pushed aside to the other side of the earth was the planet's equilibrium restored and the violence brought to an end. The imaginative Snider even provided a map showing the continents huddled together in their preflood positions. He also cited such modern evidence as similarities in fossils and geological strata found in Europe and the Americas to show that these landmasses had once been joined.

Others who puzzled over the fit of the Atlantic coastlines expanded upon a proposal made by George Darwin, son of the great evolutionist Charles Darwin. To account for the birth of the moon, the younger Darwin calculated that the young earth was spinning so rapidly that a mass of material broke free and flew out into space. Besides forming the earth's large satellite, the calamity left behind a huge cavity, at the site of what is now the Pacific Ocean. As fresh earthly material rushed into the void, other scientists speculated, the great avalanche dragged the Americas away from Africa and Europe and created the matching coastlines.°

By the end of the nineteenth century, the Austrian geologist Eduard Suess had noticed many geological similarities among the southern continents, especially the widespread distribution of fossils of an ancient fern called *Glossopteris*. He was so impressed by this evidence that he fitted the southern continents

---

°Darwin's theory was firmly buried when analysis of samples brought back from the moon by the Apollo astronauts showed that the lunar rock was essentially different in composition from terrestrial material and far older than any rocks from the Pacific basin.

together into a single landmass named Gondwanaland, after the province of Gondwana in east central India, home of the aboriginal Gonds tribe, where many *Glossopteris* fossils had been found.

Still, in spite of such clues, the majority of geologists in Wegener's lifetime were no more inclined to believe in continental drift than in a flat earth. His concept, although buttressed by modern evidence rather than by passages from the Bible, sounded like another wishful exercise in catastrophism. And by then catastrophism was in disrepute. It had given way to a new geological dogma: the principle of uniformitarianism, pioneered by the Scottish geologists James Hutton and Charles Lyell.

The name was a tongue twister, but the basic idea was simple. Certainly, local calamities like an earthquake or volcanic eruption could cause abrupt changes in the landscape. But on a global scale, the earth's surface was being remade much more slowly and uniformly. The agents of change were not sweeping catastrophes, like the Biblical flood, but steady and unrelenting processes: the grinding down of a mountainside by wind and rain, the crumbling of a rocky cliff by the pounding of the surf, the depositing of layer upon layer of sediment by swiftly flowing rivers and streams.

The pioneers of this new view of the earth also vastly extended the planet's history. They concluded that the earth was being changed so gradually that it had to be much older than the few thousand years suggested by the Bible. The miracles observed by Hutton and Lyell in the rocky scenery of Scotland and elsewhere could only have been wrought over many millions of years. In their theories, they had no place for catastrophism.

Aside from its long link with catastrophism, continental drift irritated Wegener's contemporaries for another reason. In his writings, he spoke of the "horizontal displacement" of continents. But most earth scientists said that the continents could only have moved vertically. Their reasoning was based on the prevailing concept of a cooling earth. As the earth radiated its internal heat and contracted after its fiery birth, they explained, some land sank to form ocean basins and some was squeezed up to create mountains. Never were the continents shuffled sideways.

The discovery of radioactivity, as noted in Chapter 4, had already cast doubt on this particular version of earth history. Rather than cooling off, the earth's interior might still be quite hot, perhaps even getting hotter from the radioactive elements inside it. But most scientists are a conservative sort. They are not easily turned from prevailing dogma, especially if it seems to explain nature's puzzles satisfactorily. Wegener, they said, should tend to his own business: the study of the atmosphere.

Yet he was not so easily silenced. Though personally genial and slow to anger, Wegener was fiercely stubborn in defending ideas he considered fundamentally sound. The attacks on his scientific judgment only spurred him on, even to the point of chancing another expedition to Greenland.

As it happens, Wegener did not seem especially well cast in the role of scientific prophet. He was not fiery or arrogant. Nor did he have any illusions about his abilities. He acknowledged he had no great gifts in mathematics, physics, or any other science. But he did have an unerring instinct for getting at the heart of a problem. In his work he stressed simplicity and brushed off complex formulas as something professors used to perplex their students.

Born in Berlin in 1880, a Protestant clergyman's son, Wegener studied at the universities of Heidelberg, Innsbruck, and Berlin.

From the last institution, he received a doctorate in astronomy. His astronomical research was historically interesting but of no great scientific consequence: for his thesis he converted some old, pre-Copernican tables of planetary motion into the modern decimal system. Subsequently he joined the Royal Prussian Aeronautical Observatory at Lindenberg, near Berlin, as a technical assistant. His interest switched to meteorology, in particular the physics of the upper atmosphere. The field was new; it was just beginning to attract scientific attention following the discovery of the stratosphere, a rarefied, chilly layer of air that begins at an altitude of about six miles above the earth.

More inclined to the practical side of science than the theoretical, Wegener mastered the art of flying kites and balloons in order to gather atmospheric data. He also insisted on going aloft himself. In 1906 he and his brother Kurt made a record-breaking flight in a free-floating balloon, drifting across northern Germany, Denmark, and parts of the Baltic Sea for 52½ hours.

But Wegener had dreams of more distant adventures. Even as a teen-ager, he had been smitten by the Arctic, especially Greenland, and studied its history, people, and climate. These far-off, icy regions were the frontier of the time. They were a subject of enormous popular interest, just as space is today. Thin and wiry, of only medium height, Wegener hardly looked the part of polar explorer, yet he was a man of great self-discipline and determination. He took to toughening himself by going on long hikes, climbing mountains, and learning how to ice skate and ski.

After his long and courageous balloon flight, he won a coveted place on a Danish expedition to Greenland as a meteorologist. The venture was a trial for everyone; the participants even had to haul their own sledges across the snow and ice because no dogs were available. But Wegener endured this harsh initiation into the rites of the north as well as any grizzled Arctic veteran and gained the respect of his comrades.

On his return to Germany two years later, Wegener took a junior teaching post at the University of Marburg, where he quickly became popular with his students. Not only could he make clear difficult subjects like the complex movements of the atmosphere, even writing a popular treatise on the subject, but he was much more open and accessible than the typical German university professor of the period. Later, when Wegener became the center of the great storm over continental drift, his students were said to be so loyal to their teacher that they were ready to battle with their fists anyone who maligned him.

Legend has it that Wegener got the idea for continental drift while he was watching icebergs calve from a Greenland glacier and then drift off. The story is reminiscent of the apocryphal tale of Isaac Newton and the falling apple that supposedly inspired his theory of gravity. By Wegener's own testimony, however, the inspiration was more conventional. He said that the concept occurred to him in 1910 while he was looking at a map and noticed the similarities in Atlantic coastlines. But at least one contemporary recalled hearing Wegener talk about drift as far back as 1903.

Tantalizing as the fit of the American and African coastlines was, Wegener was much too good a scientist to depend on such tenuous evidence alone. In fact, he initially dismissed drift as totally improbable. But by 1911 he had discovered other hints. Studying records of very ancient fossils, he learned of a reptile called *Mesosaurus* (literally, "middle-sized lizard" in Greek). A ferocious-looking beast with an alligator's snout and needlelike teeth, it lived about 270 million years ago in the swampy estuaries of Brazil and South Africa. Its menacing appearance notwithstanding, as a swimmer it was hardly powerful enough to have conquered 3,000 miles of open water. Wegener wondered how an animal like *Mesosaurus* came to live in two different places an ocean apart.

Biologists had a ready explanation. They said that *Mesosaurus* made its way across the ocean by so-called land bridges—natural connections that once linked distant continents. In time, however, the bridges sank, disappearing beneath the waves, just as other landmasses were presumed to have sunk, according to prevailing earth theories. Eduard Suess himself had invoked such an explanation to account for the breakup of Gondwanaland. In his view, the southern continents did not drift apart. Rather, the land between them settled below sea level, thereby blocking animal migrations. Separated by water, colonies of the same species were left in permanent isolation from one another.

Impressive as land bridges sounded, Wegener shrewdly spotted a major flaw in the theory. It violated the old laws of buoyancy, which hold that lighter materials always float atop heavier ones. These rules were originally devised to explain the flotation of solids in liquids. But they also apply when other materials are mixed together, including seemingly inflexible rock. Over a long period, even rock acts like a fluid, and a lighter layer of rock will gradually rise above a heavier one.

By the turn of the century, these ideas had come to be applied to the earth itself under what was called the principle of isostasy (from the Greek words for "equal standing"). Geologists realized that underneath the thin covering of topsoil the continents were made of varieties of granitelike rock. On average these were significantly less dense and about 20 percent lighter than the harder basalts, or lavalike rock, of the ocean floor. Wegener pointed out that under the rules of isostasy, the continents, being lighter, had to rest on top of the heavier ocean bottom, almost like logs floating in water. To him, talk of sunken land bridges was nonsense. As fragments of continental-type rock, they could no more have dropped into the sea floor than could any other part of the continents.

Wegener realized, of course, that parts of the ocean bottom did occasionally become uncovered—not because the land rose but because sea level fell during ice ages. For reasons still unknown, global temperatures periodically drop. When that happens, the polar caps expand, more water is locked up in the ice, and the oceans recede. Some shallow seas, in fact, become bone dry, creating temporary land bridges. One example is the Bering Sea, a narrow body of water between Asia and North America. It drained so completely during the last glaciation, and perhaps during earlier ones as well, that people from Siberia streamed across it into Alaska and the rest of the Americas to become the first human occupants of the New World.

But such short-lived spans could never bridge the great oceans. With a mean depth of more than two miles, the oceans would not be affected by a relatively slight drop in sea level. There had to be another way to account for the presence of *Mesosaurus* fossils on two far-flung continents. The only plausible explanation, in Wegener's eyes, was that South America and Africa were once joined. When they broke apart, they simply transported the animals along with them.

Wegener also came upon other powerful arguments for continental drift. Studying geological maps of the Old and New Worlds, he noticed that if he imagined the continents as side by side, their mountain ranges would form almost continuous chains. The Cape Mountains in South Africa, for instance, made a nearly perfect connection with the Sierras south of Buenos Aires, located across the Atlantic in Argentina. Matches could also be made between mountain ranges in eastern Canada and in Scotland and Norway. Their rock was not only of the same type but of similar age. Even their strata seemed to be laid down in the same order. Wegener offered a compelling analogy: "It is just as if we were to refit the torn pieces of a newspaper by matching their edges, then check whether or not the lines of print run smoothly across." (In piecing together the continents, Wegener anticipated the practice of modern scientists: he did not use their visible coastline but the edge of the continental shelf. Sloping gently under the sea, the shelf is a natural extension of the continent, and its outer margin, which drops sharply to the ocean bottom, constitutes the continent's true boundary.)

By 1912 Wegener felt that he had gathered enough evidence in support of continental drift to give a public lecture on it to the German Geological Society in Frankfurt. And he might have continued his researches, except for other pressing claims on his time. Returning from Greenland in 1913, he promptly married Else Köppen, the daughter of the pioneering meteorologist Vladimir Peter Köppen, famous for his system of classifying climate. Wegener would eventually succeed his father-in-law as director of the meteorological research department of the German Marine Observatory near Hamburg. But the outbreak of World War I interrupted his scientific pursuits. Although Wegener worried about the war's effect on future international scientific cooperation, he reported for duty as a reserve officer and took part in the German advance into Belgium. Early in the fighting, he was struck in the arm by a bullet. He recovered rapidly, but shortly after his return to the front he was wounded in the neck. The second injury knocked him out of action for the duration.

His convalescence gave him plenty of time to think further about continental drift. In 1915 he unveiled his reflections in his book *The Origin of Continents and Oceans*. The work was

Wegener's major exposition of his theory. Eventually it would go through four editions, appear in numerous foreign languages, and become a classic of its kind. Even today it makes intriguing reading for students of the earth sciences.

Though written in dry, scientific language, the book was a bold leap of the imagination. In its pages, Wegener journeyed 300 million years back in time to what geologists call the Carboniferous, or coal-forming, period. Neither man nor any other mammal had yet appeared on the planet. Looking out upon his re-created earth, Wegener saw not today's scattered continents but a single landmass, a continent of continents that he christened Pangaea (from the Greek words for "whole earth"). It was surrounded by an ocean that Wegener called Panthalassa (or "universal sea").

For about 100 million years Pangaea remained intact as a single landmass. But at the start of the Jurassic period, some 200 million to 150 million years ago, Wegener's supercontinent began cracking, like a great sheet of ice. On Pangaea's southern flanks, a huge slab started to pull away. Soon this block, too, would break up, forming what would become Antarctica, Australia, and the Indian subcontinent. Fifty million years later, or about 100 million years ago, during the Cretaceous peroid, when the first flowering plants appeared, another momentous change began: Africa and the Americas began breaking away from Pangaea as well. Finally, about a million years ago (a recent moment

---

Gradual breakup of Pangaea as envisioned by Wegener, starting 300 million years ago (top), continuing through opening of the Atlantic 200 million years ago (middle), and ending with the severing of the Americas 2 million years ago (bottom). Wegener's timetable was wrong, but his underlying idea was correct: the continents have drifted apart.

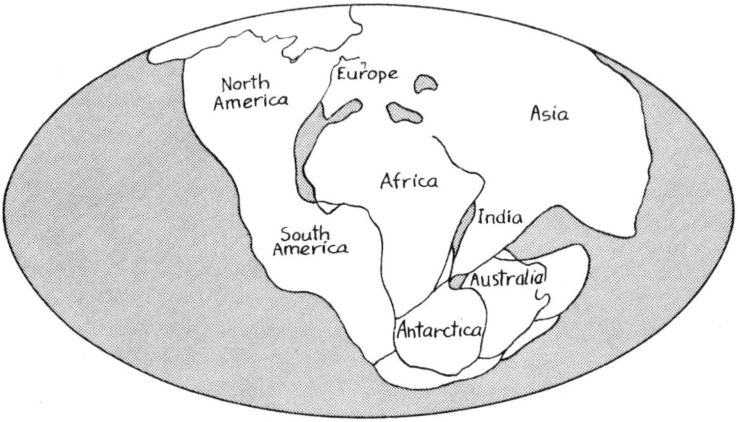
North America
Europe
Asia
Africa
India
South America
Australia
Antarctica

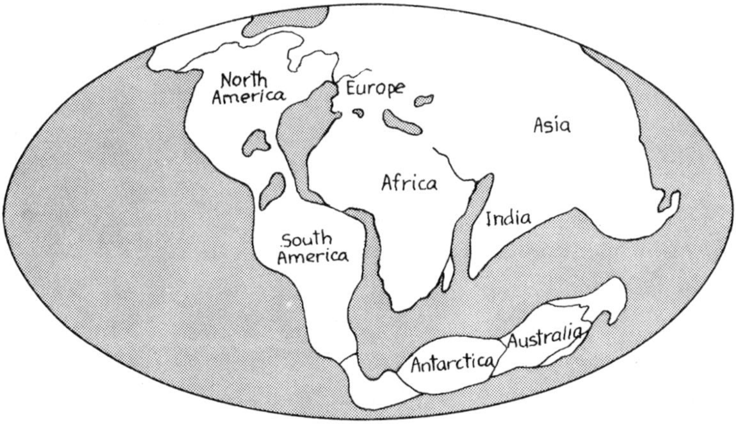
North America
Europe
Asia
Africa
India
South America
Australia
Antarctica

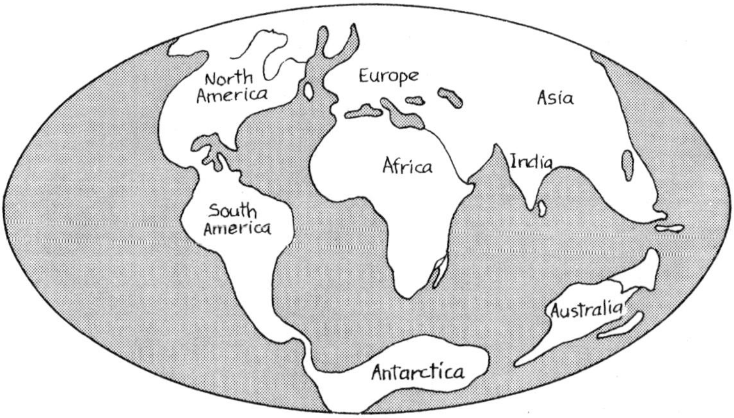
North America
Europe
Asia
India
Africa
South America
Australia
Antarctica

on the scale of geological time), the future Canada, Greenland, and Scandinavia tore away from each other.

Wegener did not stop with the earth's past. He said that the continents were still wandering, still changing the earth's visage, even if at a rate too slow to be observed in the daily course of human life.

This remarkable script simultaneously solved some of geology's most troubling problems—the curious match of distant coastlines, the dispersion of related plants and animals on widely separated continents, even the presence of such vestiges of tropical life as fossilized palms in cold realms like Norway and Antarctica. Continental drift was the key to unraveling all these mysteries, though Wegener did need a little help from another controversial geophysical possibility. He assumed that Scandinavia and Antarctica had moved into colder latitudes not only because of drift but because of changes in the earth's axis of rotation—that is, a wandering of the poles.

Most important of all, Wegener's theory finally provided a plausible explanation for the formation of mountain ranges. No longer was it necessary to rely on so dubious a proposition as a shrinking earth. Instead, Wegener said, mountains were created as the continents pushed through the ocean floor like icebreakers struggling through a frozen sea. Encountering more and more resistance, their leading edges crumpled, folded back, and were thrust up. One instance of such mountain-building could be found on the western coast of the Americas, where a westward drift of the continent had pushed up the Andes and the Rockies. Wegener also said that mountains were formed when one continent bumped into another. The most recent example was India's collision with Asia. That crunching meeting resulted in the Himalayas, the world's youngest and highest mountains, which are still believed to be growing a few inches every year because of India's northerly drift.

In his day, Wegener's thesis itself created a mountain of opposition. Fellow scientists dismissed the alleged fit of opposing coastlines as either a coincidence or an exaggeration. They charged he knew far too little about ancient fossils to draw any conclusions from them and laughingly suggested that the relatively fragile continents could no more cut through hard oceanic basalt than a saw made of soft iron could slice through tough steel. They accused Wegener of vastly overstating his case. At Greenland's alleged rate of drift, the continents would have raced around the earth 200 times since Pangaea's breakup. During a landmark symposium on continental drift in New York in 1926, one critic charged that Wegener was so prone to gather only facts in support of his idea, while ignoring all others, that he ended up "in a state of auto-intoxication."

One reason for this ferocious opposition was that Wegener was not really considered professionally qualified to speak out on matters outside meteorology. He had the bad luck of belonging to what one scientist called "the wrong trade union."

The most devastating criticism, however, came from the lordly dean of British geophysics, Sir Harold Jeffreys. And it was not based on scientific snobbery. As the "motor" for his moving continents, Wegener had relied on two energy sources: one was the gravitational tug of the moon and sun—that is, tidal drag, which he said was giving the continents a westerly push; the other was the earth's spin, which he said caused them to "flee" from the poles toward the equator. With only a few simple calculations, Jeffreys showed that these forces had only a millionth of the power necessary to move a continent, if in fact it could be budged.

Wegener acknowledged the shortcomings of some of his ideas, especially the inadequacy of his mechanism for continental drift. "The Newton of drift theory has not yet appeared," he wrote in the final edition of his book. But he had no doubt that the idea would ultimately prevail. He spent so much time trying to find convincing evidence that he was repeatedly denied a regular professorship in a German university because he was thought to be too preoccupied with subjects outside his chosen field of meteorology. Not until he was 44 years old did he win a professorial chair—at the University of Graz in Austria.

While the argument raged over drift, Wegener decided to organize one more expedition to Greenland. The main objective, to be sure, was meteorological. To monitor the cold winds sweeping down from Greenland, he planned to set up a station in the very heart of the icy plateau that would make observations through the polar winter. To measure the thickness of Greenland's icecap, he would use a relatively new and hardly danger-free technique: echo sounding, which involved lugging explosive charges across the ice and detonating them. By clocking how long it took sound waves from the blasts to bounce off the underlying rock, the scientists could tell just how far down the ice extended—if the charges did not misfire. Still, Wegener could not forget his great obsession. During the visit to Greenland, which he realized might well be his last, he was determined to collect more evidence for continental drift, in particular new and more accurate longitude readings. In this way, he hoped to convince the doubters of Greenland's westerly movement.

There were problems from the start. Even before the expedition sailed off in the summer of 1930, it was almost canceled for lack of funds. For weeks storms and ice on the Greenland coast delayed the unloading of equipment and supplies, including propeller-driven sledges. (These turned out to be failures.) By dint of makeshift construction and a heroic effort in the face of the impending darkness, Wegener's team managed to erect a temporary hut at the site of the inland weather observatory. But if the two men at the lonely outpost were to survive through the Arctic winter, they would need to be supplied with more fuel and food.

On September 21, 1930, Wegener set out with a party of 14 men and 4,000 pounds of supplies. He hoped to reach the station before it was enclosed by the long polar night, when the sun never peers over the horizon. Almost immediately, the men were blasted by fierce winds, driving snow, and unseasonable cold. After 100 miles of trekking, most of the native Greenlanders in Wegener's group turned back. Struggling on by themselves, Wegener and two companions reached the outpost five weeks later but with only a fraction of the original provisions. One man's feet were so badly frostbitten he was forced to stay behind at the station for the winter. Three men now had to make do with supplies barely adequate for two.

Wegener was anxious to get back to the base camp before the weather worsened. Early the next morning, he and a Greenlander named Rasmus Willumsen started out for the coast, 250 miles away. It was November 1, Wegener's fiftieth birthday. They had two sledges and 17 dogs. In his diary, one of the station's scientists noted grimly: "With their dogs pretty well worn out, it is a race with death." The words were prophetic. Neither Wegener nor his companion was ever seen alive again.

Some six months later, after spring arrived, Wegener's body was discovered on the trail halfway between the mid-ice station and the coast. He had apparently died of a heart attack, perhaps brought on by the tremendous exertion of battling the elements. He was buried by his companion, who marked the grave with Wegener's skis. The Greenlander appears to have continued toward the base but presumably also died en route. His body was never found.

After the death of its major advocate, interest in continental drift declined. A few scientists tried to keep Wegener's theory alive, notably the Scottish geologist Alexander Holmes. Trying to overcome Jeffreys's objections with an alternative mechanism for moving the continents, Holmes suggested that they were carried by slowly swirling flows of softened rock in the earth's mantle, in a layer directly under the crust. The possibility of such convection currents, stirred by the earth's inner heat, is now widely accepted by scientists. But in the years after Wegener's death, the efforts of Holmes and others to salvage his ideas were largely unsuccessful.

During the 1930s and 1940s, whenever geologists mentioned continental drift at all, it was usually with derision. Particularly in colleges and universities in the United States, professors held it up to their students as an object lesson in scientific blundering: using superficial evidence (the supposed fit of the continents) to draw an unwarranted conclusion (that they move). Arguments for drift were treated with about as much seriousness as astrology or flying saucers. Wegener himself became a forgotten footnote in the history of science.

That was unfortunate. Had Wegener lived to a grand old age, he would have witnessed an astonishing reversal in scientific attitudes and heard himself proclaimed a scientific prophet. By the 1960s, after a succession of dazzling discoveries—many of them by seismologists—Wegener's picture of the earth got belated confirmation. The continents did move, after all.

Wegener, as he himself probably suspected, was quite wrong

in the precise mechanism of motion. The continents did not push through oceanic bedrock but rather were rafted along by it, as Holmes had suggested. He also made something of a mess of his dates. In Wegener's world view, the continents were more or less clustered together as recently as 50 million years ago. In fact, Pangaea's breakup probably began about 200 million years ago. Nor were the continents galloping along at the pace he envisioned for Greenland; at most they averaged only a few centimeters a year. But on the major point, Wegener was absolutely right: the continents are not forever locked in place but drift about the face of the earth. And in the process, as this visionary foresaw, they cause all sorts of geological mischief, not the least of which is earthquakes.

6 pRObiNq THE plANET

Like Alfred Wegener, Andrija Mohorovičić refused to be tied to a single scientific discipline. Born in 1857 in the Balkan state of Croatia, which is now part of Yugoslavia, he embarked on a career in meteorology and pursued it with considerable distinction. By the age of 35, he had become director of the University of Zagreb's meteorological observatory. But he also was intrigued by scientific questions outside his own speciality. Inspired by the work of Milne and other pioneering seismologists, Mohorovičić (pronounced moh-HO-row-VITCH-ick) added the study of earthquakes to the observatory's activities.

However, it was not science alone that stimulated his interest in seismology. Yugoslavia, sitting astride a seismically active area, is frequently rattled by earthquakes, some of them extremely destructive. Mohorovičić, who was as anxious to help his countrymen as he was to satisfy his own scientific curiosity, realized that only if the forces at work during these deadly rampages were better understood could there be any hope of foretelling when an earthquake might strike. Thus, when a small quake shook Zagreb, the Croatian capital, in October 1909,

Mohorovičić decided to make the most of that opportunity by carefully analyzing the tremor.

He collected seismograms from more than two dozen stations up to 1,500 miles away from the epicenter. Studying the quake's vibrations, he noticed a puzzling phenomenon. There were two obviously separate groups of seismic waves, each of them traveling at a different speed. The patterns looked like the reverberations of two distinct events.

That was only the first surprise. Mohorovičić found that at a certain distance—about 125 miles—from the quake's epicenter, the second set of waves caught up with the first and overtook it. These pursuing waves behaved like aggressive race cars. Despite their slow start, they managed on the final laps to pass the pacesetters. What was Mohorovičić to make of these extraordinary observations?

By his day seismologists already knew that the zigzagging lines traced by a seismograph during an earthquake can be divided roughly into three groups. Each set of squiggles represents different types of waves that have passed through the ground from the temblor's focus. First come relatively simple waves that show up, in the markings made by the seismograph's needles, as orderly patterns of up-and-down swings. These are called primary or P waves. Then just as their swings, or amplitudes—a measure of their strength—begin to diminish, considerably larger and more powerful waves appear on the scene. These waves, characterized by greater swings of the needle, are known as secondary or S waves and totally overwhelm their predecessors. The seismogram is made even more complicated by the appearance of additional vibrations called long or L waves. They have the greatest amplitude of all.

Strength, however, is not the only feature that distinguishes one earthquake wave from another. They also differ in their fun-

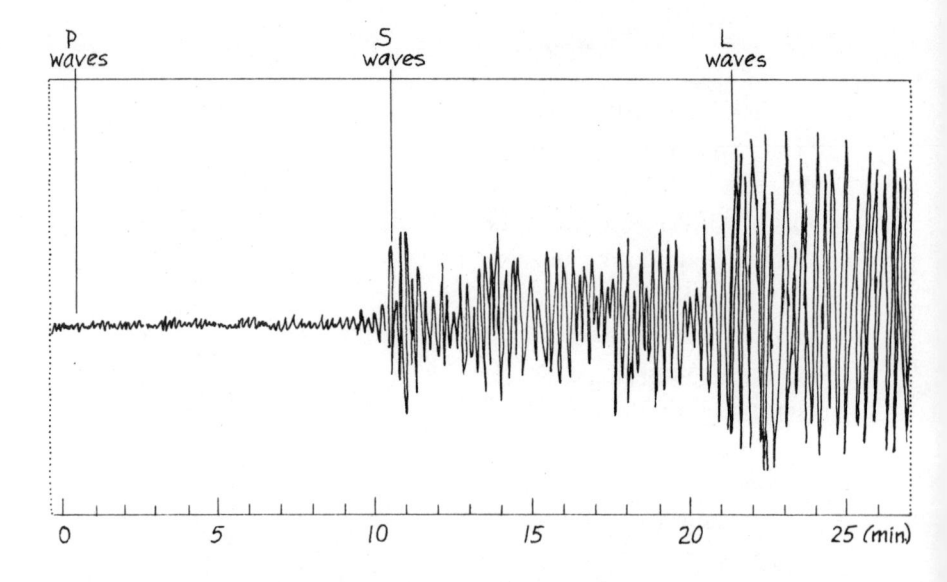

P, S, and L waves making initial appearances on a seismogram.

damental nature. P waves, for example, are the same movements of the earth that John Milne called condensational waves. They alternately compress and expand the rock—or indeed any other substance—in their path. They can travel with equal ease through a mountain of granite or the molten lava of a volcano. Even water or the gases of the atmosphere are no barrier. The jetlike roar often heard at the onset of a strong earthquake is actually a burst of P waves that has reached the earth's surface and begun to agitate the molecules of the air.

Yet the initial jolt that starts the earth quaking also moves material in another way. Instead of pushing and pulling the particles of rock back and forth in the direction of the wave's travels, it jiggles them up and down and from side to side, at right angles to the wave motion. The result is S waves, some of the earth movements that Milne grouped under the name distortional waves. If a picture could be taken of them, they would resemble the wiggles in a rope being shaken by two youngsters holding it at either end. As S waves spread out from the quake's focus, their movements are somewhat wasteful, like those of a dancer who takes a step to the side for every one forward. Consequently, S waves travel much slower than P waves. In typical rock, their velocity is about two miles per second, about half that of P waves.

Unlike their seismic cousins, S waves cannot move through fluids, which means that they are effectively blocked by water and air.° The reason is that the chemical building blocks, or molecules, of fluids are only loosely linked at best. And so if a molecule in a fluid is pushed to the side in the characteristic S-wave motion, it will not pull along the molecule next to it. Thus, the wave's motion is transmitted no further. (By contrast, the molecules of a solid are tightly bound together, easily letting them jiggle their neighbors.) Even so, in terms of destructiveness, there is nothing secondary about S waves. Simultaneously shaking buildings sideways and up and down, they often cause far more damage than P waves.

Together P and S waves are known as body waves because they travel mainly within the body of the earth. Yet as they radiate from a quake's focus, some will inevitably work their way out of the earth and begin vibrating the ground, creating surface waves. These are similar to the ripples that occur when a rock is tossed into a pond. Surface waves can travel enormous distances, sometimes circling the earth several times before they exhaust themselves.

Like body waves, surface waves come in two varieties. Both were predicted even before seismologists actually spotted them

---

°Scientifically speaking, gases, including those of the atmosphere, as well as liquids, are considered fluids.

in their records. In 1885 the British physicist Lord Rayleigh made calculations showing that earthquakes should produce one kind of surface wave with a circular motion like that of rolling ocean waves. Alerted to their presence, seismologists checked the tangle of markings on their seismograms, and there, just as he had said, were Rayleigh's waves.

But sophisticated instruments are not always necessary to tell the presence of these powerful waves. Rayleigh waves probably caused the surprising changes in water levels of Europe's lakes and harbors immediately after the destructive 1755 Lisbon quake. The phenomenon was first described scientifically by a Swiss investigator named F. A. Forel, who in the late nineteenth century made a systematic study of Switzerland's lakes. These picturesque, mountain-rimmed bodies of water had long been known to rise and fall rhythmically by as much as several inches at totally unexpected times. Forel gave the oscillations the French name *seiche* (pronounced SAYSH). While they can sometimes be produced by winds and storms, the breakerlike Rayleigh waves of earthquakes seem especially good at creating them, sometimes over huge distances. In 1950 Rayleigh waves from a quake in the Indian state of Assam apparently caused sharp fluctuations halfway around the world in the levels of reservoirs in England. Such long-range agitation can occur even in small bodies of water. A quake in the Aleutians is said to have so agitated the water in a Texas swimming pool that the fully clad guests gathered for a poolside party were drenched.

In 1911 the British mathematician A. E. H. Love postulated still another type of surface wave. He explained that it would shake the ground from side to side in a direction parallel to the surface, like the crawling movements of a snake. Love waves were promptly found in seismograms (though Mohorovičić did not learn of them soon enough for his study). Their arrival times at seismic stations indicated that surface waves of any type travel somewhat slower than body waves—though, of the two kinds of surface waves, Love waves are slightly faster. Unlike Rayleigh waves, however, Love waves cannot move through fluids (for the same reason that S waves cannot).

In Mohorovičić's day, scientific understanding of seismic waves was far from complete. But he knew enough about them to realize that something was seriously amiss when it appeared that the Zagreb quake had produced two different sets of P and S waves, each arriving at a different time. Pondering these perplexing observations, he reasoned that there could be only one really satisfactory explanation: some of the waves had traveled through a less compressible, firmer layer of rock under the earth's crust, which gave them a boost in speed. (Remember that Mallet had learned years earlier that seismic waves travled faster in more rigid rock.)

But how deep was this layer? And why did some waves enter it and not others? Methodical investigator that he was, Mohorovičić had used data from different stations to establish exactly where the waves originated. The quake's epicenter turned out to be Croatia's Kulpa Valley. Then he figured the distance to each of the recording stations and plotted the arrival times of the various seismic waves at the individual stations on a graph, with one axis representing time, the other distance traveled. In this way he learned that the original waves were being passed after they had traveled 125 miles from the epicenter. At any observatory beyond this distance, the second group of waves invariably arrived first.

Apparently, said Mohorovičić, it was here that the stations were starting to pick up waves from the second layer. He explained it this way: as the quake sent waves into the earth, some struck the top of the lower second layer at a steep angle and were immediately reflected back into the crust, where they continued at their usual speed. Others, however, hit at a shallower angle and were bent, or refracted, like a beam of light in a lens, into the subcrustal zone. When they finally curved back to the surface, they had covered a much greater distance. But they had also gotten such a boost in speed in the denser material that they beat out the waves whose journey was confined entirely to the crust. Mohorovičić reckoned that the critical boundary between the layers was at a depth of about 30 miles.

The investigation of the Zagreb quake was a superb example of seismological exploration. Using the earth's own vibrations as if they were X-rays, Mohorovičić had finally pinpointed the elusive zone—or discontinuity, as scientists call any abrupt change in their measurements—where the earth's crust comes to an end and the underlying mantle begins. Since Mohorovičić's original studies, other seismologists have refined his figures. Typically, under the continents, the crust is about 20 miles thick, except in mountainous regions, where, under the weight of the overlying rock, it presses down as much as 40 miles. Under the oceans, it is only about three miles thick. In honor of its discoverer, the boundary between these layers of the earth is called the Mohorovičić Discontinuity or, more mercifully, the Moho.

In the 1950s members of an informal and sometimes playful group of scientists calling themselves the American Miscellaneous Society proposed drilling deep enough into the earth to obtain a sample of the mantle. They called their scheme Project Mohole (after the Moho). But as it became clear after several test borings that the bill for this undertaking might climb to tens of millions of dollars, Congress put a stopper in Mohole and canceled any further funding for it.

By dramatically showing the value of seismic waves in revealing the earth's secrets, Mohorovičić's careful study had a profound effect on seismology. Other scientists followed in his footsteps, utilizing seismic probing in many novel and ingenious ways. Some did not even wait for earthquakes to strike. They took to creating little shocks of their own, not to find major new features within the earth but to locate isolated strata—say, those that might have trapped a pool of oil.

In 1911, only two years after Mohorovičić began his detailed examination of the Zagreb quake, a 22-year-old student at the University of Göttingen, in Germany, named Beno Gutenberg solved another major mystery about the earth's structure. When a quake occurs, waves spread out in all directions from its focus. Some of them go deep into the earth, only to emerge at its surface thousands of miles away. But at a certain distance something strange occurs. Between 7,000 miles to 9,600 miles from the focus (as measured along the earth's curved surface), there forms what seismologists call a shadow zone, which rings the earth in a 2,600-mile-wide belt. Seismographs that happen to be stationed within the globe-girdling zone are unable to pick up any waves from that particular quake. Seismically, the area is in the dark, so to speak; hence the name shadow zone. Yet just beyond the zone, some P waves start to reappear, though later than expected. S waves, however, remain conspicuously absent.

Independently, two scientists, the Irish geologist Richard D. Oldham, one of Milne's co-workers, and the German geophysicist Emil Wiechert, suggested an explanation. At the center of the planet, they said, there must be a large clump of extremely hot and dense material that acts as a seismic barrier, blocking the passage of earthquake waves. When the waves descend deep into the earth, they reach this core. Those that hit it at a glancing angle skip off, like a rock bouncing off a pond's surface. Those that strike more directly continue through it, although their path is somewhat bent toward the center of the earth, thereby creat-

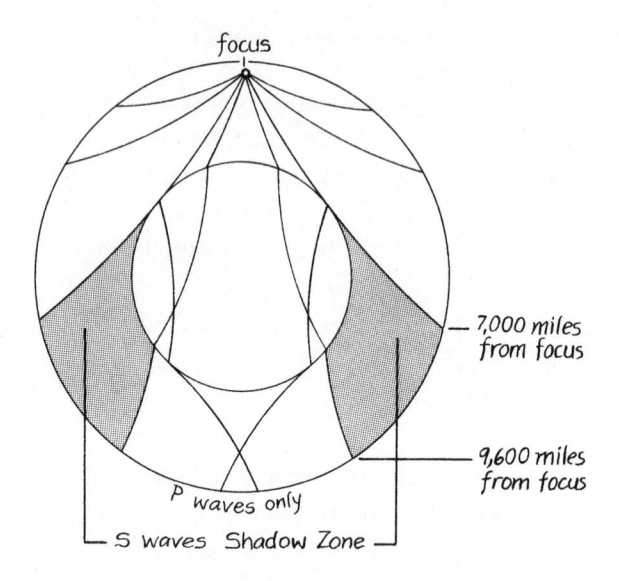

Seismic waves are blocked by the earth's liquid core at distances of 7,000 to 9,600 miles from the focus of a quake (as measured along the earth's curved surface). This creates a 2,600-mile-wide shadow zone circling earth. Just beyond this belt, some P waves begin to reappear, although later than expected because they are slowed down by the liquid.

ing a "skip" zone on the surface where no waves emerge. Still, only P waves can take this journey. Since the core is partially molten, or fluid, S waves are stopped entirely by it. Thus, on the opposite half of the earth away from the quake, there appears a seismically "dark" belt where no waves of any kind appear and another zone where only P waves are detected.

But all this was still only theory. Gutenberg's task was to prove the core's existence mathematically by fixing its dimensions as precisely as Mohorovičić had located the top of the mantle. In an era before computers that was not easy. The job involved long and tedious calculations, comparing various possible models of the earth's interior with actual seismic data. After much trial and error, Gutenberg found a match when he assumed a core that began about 1,800 miles below the earth's surface. Simple arithmetic gave him the core's size. Within the earth, itself a slightly flattened sphere 7,900 miles in diameter, there was a hot, dense ball about 4,300 miles across.

Gutenberg modestly said his figure might be wrong by as much as 60 miles. Modern measurements have shown he was off by no more than about 12 miles. His precise mathematical analysis moved the core from the category of informed speculation to the area of accepted scientific fact. As in the case of the Moho, the newly found boundary between mantle and core was named after its discoverer. It became the Gutenberg Discontinuity.

In the nineteenth century the French science-fiction writer Jules Verne had imagined a journey to the center of the earth.

A glimpse at the earth's interior shows major divisions.

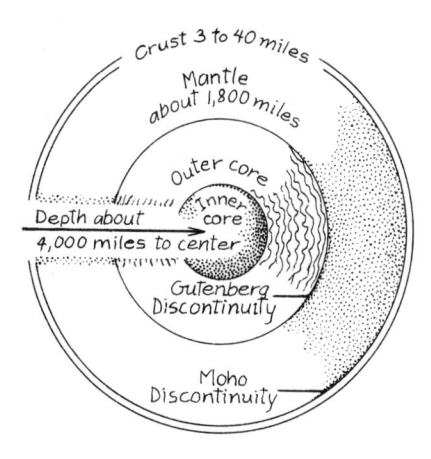

Only a few years later Mohorovičić and Gutenberg turned the fantasy into reality—not in person, of course, but by the only means available for exploring the earth's hot interior. In effect, they traveled on the waves of earthquakes, using the waves' changing velocities to discern differences in planetary structure. With their explorations, the new science of seismology had succeeded in fixing the boundaries of the earth's three major zones: crust, mantle, and core. Regions once thought to be totally beyond the pale of scientific inspection now stood plainly revealed.

Other seismologists have since found many additional details of the planet's interior. The core, for example, is not a single scalding mass, but a solid inner sphere enclosed by a molten outer layer. Still other regions where there are abrupt changes in rock density have been discovered at various depths in the mantle as well. Gutenberg himself contributed to this work. In 1926, after he had become a researcher at the University of Frankfurt, he discovered a deeper layer in the mantle at about 90 miles below the surface. In this region, seismic waves traveled about 6 percent slower than in parts of the mantle immediately under the crust. The drop in velocity was a surprise, since the layer's greater density under the weight of overlying material would presumably have made it a faster conveyor of seismic waves. But Gutenberg decided that prevailing pressures and temperatures at this depth had a different effect. The rock had lost its firm internal structure and was perhaps able to flow. One consequence of his finding was that, unlike most of his colleagues, Gutenberg was inclined to believe that continental drift was more than Alfred Wegener's crazy dream. After all, if materials within the earth moved, maybe they could carry continents with them.

In 1930 Gutenberg left Germany and began a long and productive association with the California Institute of Technology. A few years later, he joined with a Caltech colleague, Charles F. Richter, in devising the scale that has since become the standard measure for the magnitude of earthquakes. Looking for an easy way to classify the relative size of California's tremors, Richter had noticed one of those things about quakes that are so obvious they seem, in retrospect, absurdly simple: when he traced seismograms of the same quake recorded at varying distances from its epicenter on top of one another, he found that the jagged wave patterns matched in shape, if not in size. In a sense, they were like a stack of salad bowls nestled inside each other—the bigger bowls representing seismograms made closer to the quake site. Using this similarity as a yardstick, Richter and Gutenberg went on to define a baseline, or minimal, tremor against which all others could be compared. Their scale began with a quake that would move the needle of a standard seismograph stationed 100 kilometers (62 miles) from the quake's focus 1 millimeter (about four-hundredths of an inch). Since this initial work, the scale has been vastly refined and has become much more complex. But Gutenberg's role in its original development has tended to be overlooked. Some seismologists think that it should properly be called the Richter-Gutenberg scale.

Even without this honor, Gutenberg's reputation remains secure. In 1947 he became director of Caltech's famed seismological laboratory, a post he held for 11 years during a period when seismology became increasingly important. It was also a time when the scientific view of the earth was undergoing a complete revolution.

Surprisingly, the seeds of that revolution were sown not on land but on the ocean floor. For centuries geologists had concentrated on studying the bedrock directly under their feet, all the while ignoring the far greater portion of the planet's surface: the three-quarters of the area under the seas. In part they were held back by a lack of adequate tools; scientists could more easily study the surface of the moon than peer into the murky depths. But their neglect of the sea bottom was not for this reason alone. They also had some serious misconceptions about it.

For a long time many researchers considered the ocean floor scientifically uninteresting. They regarded it as nothing more than old continental material that had somehow slipped below the waves. In the few places where it had been examined, the sea bottom looked as flat, empty, and featureless as some deserts. The undersea wasteland was not covered by sand, but something that seemed just as dull: dark, oozing sediments consisting mostly of the remains of marine organisms and of muddy wastes washed off the continental shelf, the sloping, submerged regions just off shore. To many geologists, there was no point to studying such apparently barren terrain. Recalling those unenlightened years, Bruce Heezen of Columbia University's Lamont-Doherty Geological Observatory once said, "You can't imagine how primitive our knowledge [of the sea floor] was."

In fact, until relatively recently, scientists did not even really know the depths of the oceans. The Greeks, who had managed to make good scientific estimates of the earth's diameter, merely speculated that the seas were as deep as the mountains were high. In 1521 the Portuguese circumnavigator Ferdinand Magellan let out nearly half a mile of line into the Pacific and still could not reach bottom. He concluded that its depth was beyond measurement. Finally, in 1856 a surveyor named Alexander Dallas Bache solved the puzzle with the help of the big quake that rocked Japan a year before. A great-grandson of Benjamin Franklin, he cleverly used the time it had taken a tsunami—a seismic sea wave triggered by the quake—to cross the Pacific. Realizing that the velocity of the wave related both to its height, which he knew, and the ocean's depth, which was the unknown x in his equation, he calculated that the Pacific was little more than two miles deep along the tsunami's path. His measurement turned out to be only about 15 percent under the mark. His illustrious ancestor, an amateur scientist himself, would surely have been proud.

But as the twentieth century dawned, oceanographic techniques improved and new instruments were developed that enabled scientists to make measurements more directly. Especially important was the echo sounder, which worked by reflecting pulses of sound—actually P waves—off the ocean floor or the layers immediately below. Soon there began to emerge a hidden world that became more breathtaking with each click of the echo sounder. As profiles of the bottom emerged from the research vessels prowling the seas, scientists began to realize that it was not a landscape of dreary sameness, but one as exciting and varied as any onshore. There were trenches deeper than the Grand Canyon, mountains higher than Everest, and plains broader than any in Kansas.

Few of the ships that explored the sea floor in the period of stepped-up oceanographic investigations after World War II contributed more than the *Vema*. Originally a three-masted schooner built in Denmark as an elegant private yacht, she seemed destined for the scrap heap by the end of the 1940s until her rescue by oceanographer Maurice Ewing, Lamont-Doherty's founding director. Recognizing her potential as a research vessel, he removed her masts, added laboratories, and crammed every bit of extra space with scientific gear. Still, *Vema* retained her sleek lines. And for more than 25 years this scientific mistress of the seas gathered priceless information on the ocean floor, largely under Ewing's firm hand.

A geologist and oil prospector by training, the Doc, as he was called by almost everyone, did not believe much in spinning fanciful theories. Rather, he emphasized the collection of detailed data. Without such information, he liked to point out, theorizing about the earth was worthless. At first he and his colleagues did their fact-gathering by dropping satchels of explosives over

Maurice ("Doc") Ewing, founding director of Lamont-Doherty Geological Observatory, at dockside with the Vema.

Vema's sides. The blasts created seismic waves that were more powerful and thus could penetrate deeper than soundings done by other means. As the waves reflected off various layers of the sea floor, they produced what were, in effect, cross-sectional views down to a depth of several miles. Later the risks of handling TNT were eliminated by the development of a sound-wave generator that pinged continuously as it was towed safely behind the ship and the echoes from the bottom were automatically recorded. Yet perils remained. During one severe storm, Ewing was tossed overboard and narrowly escaped drowning.

But the dangers did not deter Ewing, whose passionate quest to understand the structure of the sea floor soon produced results that made the risk-taking seem worthwhile. Geologists had always regarded the oceans as one of the earth's most ancient features, as least two billion years old, perhaps much older. Because of this long history, they had expected to discover great accumulations of sediment on the sea floor. Indeed, calculations indicated that after only 100 million years, a small part of the oceans' lifetime, the sediment should have built to a thickness of a mile or so. But as the seabed surveys continued, the layers of sediment turned out to be far thinner than expected. Typically, the ocean floor was carpeted with only about 1,500 feet of sediment, a fraction of what should have been there.

The shortfall meant one of two things: either the oceans were much younger than anyone had supposed, or the sediment was being removed by some sort of natural vacuum cleaner. Both possibilities puzzled scientists. But soon they were confronted by still more surprises from the deep. As far back as the middle of the nineteenth century, primitive soundings, or depth measurements made by dropping lines over the sides of survey ships, had given hints of hilly terrain in the middle of the Atlantic. In the late 1920s, in the first extensive deep-sea use of the echo sounder, the German research vessel *Meteor* had found signs that there were actually many mountains there, but the readings were lost in the Allied bombing of Berlin during World War II. Crisscrossing these elevated areas in the 1950s, *Vema* confirmed that the Atlantic is divided by a full-scale mountain range, which became known as the Mid-Atlantic Ridge. In some areas, Ewing and his colleagues discovered what seemed to be deep gullies, which he said might be faults linked with the many undersea earthquakes that rocked the ridge. Turning the plethora of new data into detailed charts of the ocean floor, Lamont geographer Marie Tharp showed that the ridge itself is bisected by a huge valley, up to 30 miles wide and more than a mile deep.

Following in *Vema*'s wake, research vessels from other institutions found submerged mountain ranges in other oceans as well. Like the Mid-Atlantic Ridge, these rugged belts are divided by central rift zones, or valleys, which are the site of intense heat flows. Water samples taken from the depths directly above the rifts are significantly warmer than those collected elsewhere on the bottom. One possible clue to the mysterious heating lay in the ridge's periodic volcanic eruptions, such as the one that created the island of Surtsey, off the coast of Iceland, in 1963. There was obviously some sort of natural cauldron stirring under these mountains.

From new and more sensitive seismological stations onshore came another tantalizing finding. Established to detect distant nuclear blasts, they could pinpoint earthquakes—natural or man-made—almost anywhere, even under the seas. One byproduct of this added capability was the discovery that most undersea quakes are occurring in the very heart of the rift valleys, usually at a depth of less than 20 miles.

After studying these seismic patterns, Ewing and Heezen made a bold prediction. They said that wherever quakes frequently shake the seabed, scientists would find submerged mountain belts like the Mid-Atlantic Ridge. They would extend around the earth in an unbroken chain some 40,000 miles long and reach into all the seas. If Ewing and Heezen were right, the mountains would represent an earthly feature of unprecedented size, the largest geographical discovery since the icebound shores of Antarctica were first glimpsed by early nineteenth-century sealers and whalers.

The proof came quickly. Excited by the new findings, scientists had organized the International Geophysical Year of 1957–1958. It was the largest multinational investigation ever undertaken of the planet's oceans and atmosphere. Research vessels of every major country roamed the seas, accumulating a vast store of information. They found that the ridge system makes its way through every ocean, from the polar seas in the north and south, around the Pacific, and across the Indian Ocean. The Columbia researchers called the winding chain of submerged mountains the Mid-Ocean Ridge.

There were major surprises in other parts of the sea floor as well. Like iron-bearing minerals on land, the ocean rock retains an imprint of the magnetic field that prevailed at the time it cooled off and hardened, almost as if tiny magnets had been left inside. Yet as oceanographers studied the readings from the sensitive magnetometers—devices for measuring the strength of a magnetic field—that they towed behind their ships over the sea floor, they found disconcerting patterns. In some places, the ancient magnetism seemed to be exceptionally strong; in others, weak. From their study of such fossil magnetism in land rocks, scientists had learned that in ages past the earth's magnetic field had occasionally flip-flopped, so that if there had been any compasses around then, their needles would have pointed south instead of north. But the ancient magnetic patterns on the ocean floor seemed to be thoroughly irregular and confusing, unlike anything seen in the land rocks.

Also measured by the oceanographers were fluctuations in the pull of the earth's gravity in different parts of the ocean. Such readings indicate variations in the density of the underlying rock—the more compact the material, the greater the gravitational tugging. The variations were slight, to be sure, and only detectable by very precise instruments. But as far back as the late 1920s and the 1930s, a Dutch geophysicist named Felix Andries Vening Meinesz had squeezed his massive frame into the tight quarters of a submarine and taken such readings. Perplexingly, he learned that gravity is noticeably weaker over the oceanic trenches, which are great chasms found at the edge of some continents and island chains, than in other parts of the sea. Eventually it became apparent to scientists that the earth's crust is somehow being pulled—or pushed—into these abysses, which reach a depth of almost seven miles near the Marianas Islands in the Pacific. But the gravitational anomalies detected by Vening Meinesz, as well as by later researchers, were too small to account for the downward thrusting. Some other forces had to be drawing the crust into the earth.

Still other complications had turned up in the seabed. During World War II, as commander of a United States navy transport ship that shuttled between the islands of the Pacific, Princeton geologist Harry H. Hess found that he had plenty of time on his hands during the uneventful voyages. So he decided to do a little ocean surveying. By keeping the ship's echo sounder working at all times, he was able to obtain a continuous profile of the ocean floor along the vessel's track.

Routinely scanning the machine's rolls of printouts one day, he spotted what looked like an undersea mountain whose top had been chopped off. Subsequently Hess located 20 more of these strange truncated peaks. Other scientists eventually found hundreds of others. They turned out to be a type of seamount, or volcano, that had drowned in the sea. Hess called them guyots (pronounced GHEE-ohs, with a hard g, as in glee), in honor of his mentor, Arnold H. Guyot, Princeton's first geologist. Once they had apparently stood out of the water, like the volcanically formed islands of Hawaii. Now they were submerged, their upper portions eroded by the waves. Later, oceanographers discovered that the farther guyots are from volcanically active areas, the more worn down and ancient they are likely to be. These volcanoes appeared to have been carried across the sea floor, often many miles from their birthplaces.

Even as these explorations were going on at sea, seismologists did some long-distance probing from shore. By carefully noting the location of every quake detected in the seabed, they found that almost all were occurring either along the ridges or under the trenches. The latter type were especially intriguing. Many rippled the earth at extreme depths, sometimes as far down as 400 miles. This fact was contrary to all expectations: scientists thought that the earth was so thoroughly molten at these levels of its interior, far below the crust and well into the mantle, that it could not possibly fracture.

Another surprise came when the researchers plotted the varying depths of the mantle quakes on charts, representing each quake's focus with a dot. The markings formed a sharply angled line that pointed like a dagger into the earth. On the Asian side of the Pacific, under the trench off the Japanese archipelago, the line inclined westward toward the mainland; off the coast of South America, it veered toward the east under that continent. Similar patterns were found under other Pacific trenches, notably the one off the Tonga Islands between New Zealand and Samoa, another site of frequent deep-sea quakes. Incredibly, the entire Pacific basin seemed to form one grand circle of earthquake activity.

Some inkling of the sloping angle formed by earthquakes under the trenches had already come from the pioneering work of the Japanese seismologist Kiyoo Wadati in the late 1920s and 1930s. While studying the patterns of earthquakes in the seabed off Japan, near the Japan trench, Wadati discovered that the deeper the quakes were occurring, the closer they were to the Asian mainland. In 1954 the noted Caltech seismologist Hugo Benioff attempted an explanation of these unusual seismic patterns by suggesting that huge slabs of ocean floor were thrusting downward into the mantle. He could not say what caused the subduction, as this phenomenon came to be called. But he figured its consequences were momentous. It created the trenches and caused the quakes beneath them. It also produced such enormous pressures that there was a vast buildup of heat, thus fueling the volcanoes that have risen all along the Pacific's rim.

Despite Benioff's considerable reputation, many scientists scoffed at his ideas. They could no more believe that parts of the earth's crust were being swallowed up in the trenches than that the continents were in motion. If pieces of the crust were in fact vanishing, something had to be replacing the missing material. But what? And where? Benioff could not say, yet he had come startlingly close to explaining the seismic activity under the seas and, along the way, rescuing Wegener's long-forgotten ideas from oblivion. Soon Benioff's theorizing would be confirmed, and the understanding of earthquakes would take another giant stride forward.

7 THE VISIONARIES PREVAIL

As he showed by his discovery of guyots during World War II, Harry Hess was an extremely dedicated and gifted earth scientist. Returning to Princeton after his navy service, he became chairman of the university's geology department and one of the more influential scientists in the United States, often called upon to advise the government on major scientific projects. But what especially distinguished Hess was his verve and imagination. Unlike all too many senior scientists, he was not afraid of entertaining unconventional or even radical scientific ideas.

One instance of this aspect of Hess's character was his membership in the American Miscellaneous Society, the free-spirited and informal group of scientists that proposed Project Mohole. Still another example was his willingness to give a hearing to an extremely controversial scientific figure, Immanuel Velikovsky. In the 1950s the Russian-born physician and psychoanalyst had set off a storm with the publication of his bestselling book *Worlds in Collision*. In this and succeeding works, Velikovsky used a hodgepodge of ancient myths and modern science to argue that a large comet had torn free from the giant planet Jupiter, narrowly missed hitting Mars and the earth, then settled into an orbit as the planet Venus. The near-calamitous encounters, Velikovsky insisted, occurred not in the primordial past, when such collisions may well have taken place, but only a few thousand years ago. In his view they accounted for miraculous Biblical events like the draining of the Red Sea, the apparent stopping of the sun cited in the Book of Joshua ("Sun, stand thou upon Gibeon"), and the rain of life-sustaining manna from the heavens that nourished the Israelites during their wanderings through the Sinai wilderness. The manna, said Velikovsky, consisted of hydrocarbons from the comet's tail.

Hess, of course, recognized that Velikovsky's ideas violated almost every sacred principle of modern physics and astronomy. There is, for instance, no evidence that Venus has traveled anywhere else except in its current orbital path for millions of years. But Hess was convinced that scientific truth is best served, not by squelching unorthodox theories, but by exposing them to the full light of critical public examination. At least partly in this spirit, he tossed a scientific bombshell of his own.

The explosion came in a 1962 paper that Hess innocuously titled "History of Ocean Basins." To a certain extent, it was nothing more than a synthesis of much of what had been learned about the sea floor during the previous decade of intensive oceanographic exploration. But entwined in the dry technical discussion was a stunningly bold theme. Hess said that Wegener was basically right. The continents did drift, although in a way quite different than he had imagined.

Hess began his account of the ocean basins by retracing the history of the earth itself. No one knows the precise details of that great unwitnessed drama 4.6 billion years ago. They can only be inferred from mathematical models and the study of such things as moon rocks and meteorites, objects that still bear the scars of those cataclysmic years. But there is general agreement among scientists that the earth was formed out of the myriad small fragments in the great cloud of dust and gases swirling around the young sun. As these bits and pieces of cosmic debris collided, the earth became larger and larger, as did the other objects in the inner solar system, including the moon. Still, this scenario, which was largely the work of the chemist Harold Urey, left unsolved a major scientific mystery: how did the moon and earth fall into their celestial dance that has left one orbiting the other? Urey himself inclined to the "brother" theory: that both bodies were born almost simultaneously in the same cosmic neighborhood and have been gravitationally locked together ever since.

In Urey's view of genesis, the earth was born relatively cold, as opposed to the belief of nineteenth-century scientists that it was a ball of fire spun off by the sun. However, its temperature soon started climbing. The original collisions themselves had produced heat. Heat was also rapidly building up from the young earth's stockpile of radioactive materials. After a billion years or so, the earth's interior began to melt. Then came what Hess called, in ringing, mock-Velikovskian tones, the "great catastrophe." Heavier elements, mostly iron and nickel, sank swiftly in a molten mass to form the earth's core. Somewhat lighter materials, like silica, became the mantle and crust. The lightest stuff of all settled on the planet's thin outer surface, floating atop the crust like pieces of toast in a bowl of soup. This granitelike slag formed the lighter rock of the original continental mass.

In short, the earth's internal structure had been rapidly reorganized by a huge convection current. Such currents are nothing more than heat-driven movements like those in a simmering pot of cereal. As the cereal cooks over the flame, it expands, rises in the pot's center, and spreads at the top. After cooling and contracting, it sinks back down along the pot's sides, only to be reheated and to begin the cycle anew. Hess envisioned the initial reshuffling of material within the earth as a single global current. But as the earth's core expanded, he said, movements within the mantle became constrained. The original current broke into a number of smaller convection "cells," each of them in effect a separate pot. Now there were several places where heated rock rose up through the mantle, broke through the crust, pushed outward, and eventually sank.

This script, as Hess acknowledged, was not original. Years earlier a few bold geologists, notably Arthur Holmes, had postulated the existence of convection currents within the earth as a possible "motor" for continental drift. But they had no proof. Hess's shrewd insight was to find the missing evidence among the recent discoveries on the ocean floor. Hints of convection currents, he said, were there for all to see—at the mid-ocean ridges, down the yawning depths of the deep-sea trenches with their weakened gravity, in the surprisingly thin layer of sea-floor sediment, and in the relatively young age of ocean rocks.

The possibility of fluidlike movements within the earth stretched the scientific imagination. Every indication is that the stuff of the mantle is as hard as any rock on the earth's surface. It even fractures to produce earthquakes, although geophysicists as yet did not understand why that should happen so deep within the earth. But the hardness of rock can be deceiving. Materials scientists have long known that even such brittle substances as ice slowly deform and flow under continuous pressure. And what was driving the currents? Like Holmes, Hess had the terrestrial pot being stirred by radioactive heating. But the movements, he said, are extremely slow. The ascent of material to the surface takes millions of years, although the tempo picks up when parts of the mantle finally break through the crust as

The Visionaries Prevail

lava at the mid-ocean ridges. There the rock rapidly cools and hardens, attaches itself to existing rock on either side of the ridge, and turns into the familiar basalt of the ocean floor. But still more mantle is pressing upward. Pushed from below, the freshly formed sea floor continues its lumbering journey, moving outward in opposite directions away from the ridge, like the spreading cereal in the pot. If lighter continental material happens to be sitting on top of it, it will be carried along as well, like parcels riding on what Holmes called "an endless traveling [conveyor] belt."

But what the earthly conveyor belt brings up, it must eventually carry back down. Otherwise the seabed would grow indefinitely. Many millions of years later the moving ocean floor arrives at the trenches, where it is swallowed up by the earth and reabsorbed into the mantle for another run through this age-old convection cycle. Only the continents, floating on top of the heavier sea floor, are spared total destruction, although they may be battered and pummeled and squished together as they ride their oceanic magic carpet. Concluded Hess: "The earth is a dynamic body with its surface constantly changing."

These new ideas became known as the theory of sea-floor spreading, a name given them by geophysicist David S. Dietz, who published a similar paper at about the same time. Although Hess is usually given chief credit because his article had already been widely circulated among geologists prior to its formal publication, Dietz added a particularly intriguing wrinkle. He said that the crust moved together with the hard, topmost layer of the mantle as one 40-mile-thick "plate" while it was spreading from the ridges and descending into the trenches. Reviving an old geological term, he called the plate the lithosphere (after the Greek word for "rock"). And he said this hard layer of rock slid on a somewhat softer part of the mantle called the asthenosphere

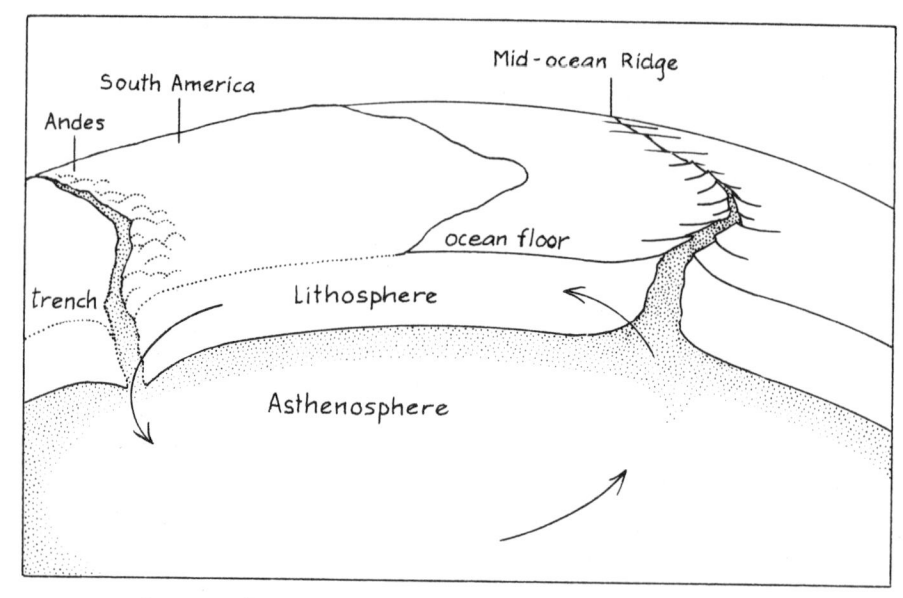

Mechanism of continental drift. Hot mantle material rises through crust at mid-ocean ridge, creating new sea floor. As the freshly created crustal material moves away from the ridge, it carries continents along with it like parcels on a conveyor belt. Finally, the sea floor, as well as its continental cargo, presses back into the earth's interior at deep-sea trenches for renewal of age-old cycle.

(from the Greek for "weak"). Dietz's ideas were a shrewd premonition of a startling concept that would shake the earth sciences five years later: the theory of plate tectonics, which holds that the entire outer surface of the earth is composed of a cap of large and small plates constantly jostling, bumping, grinding, and pulling away from each other in a slow-motion geological dance.

The Hess-Dietz hypothesis overcame two major objections to Wegener's old drift concepts. It provided a plausible propulsive force—convection currents within the earth—and it moved the continents in a geologically acceptable way. They did not plow

The Visionaries Prevail

through the hard, dense ocean floor, as Wegener had tried to argue, even though continental rocks are less dense and inherently weaker. Rather they were carried along by the moving seabed, almost like logs in a flowing stream.

Aware of the speculative nature of these ideas, Hess cautiously called his paper "an essay in geopoetry." But additional support was not long in coming. Scientists already knew, as noted (see Chapter 6), that the earth's magnetic field periodically flips over, so that the north magnetic pole becomes the south pole and vice versa. Indeed, studies of the ocean floor by scientists from the Lamont-Doherty Observatory would soon show that no fewer than 171 reversals had occurred in the past 76 million years. (The last took place about 700,000 years ago and the next is overdue.) Some scientists have even linked the mass extinction of certain animals, including the dinosaurs, to magnetic reversals. One such doomsday scenario goes as follows: as the reversal approaches, the strength of the earth's magnetism declines and the protective wall of magnetism around the planet weakens, exposing its surface to a flood of lethal high-energy radiation from space. Still another cataclysmic sequence ties magnetic reversals to changes in the earth's spin axis. According to this controversial suggestion, such wobbling might trigger worldwide earthquakes and volcanic eruptions, inject enormous amounts of dust into the atmosphere, and so drastically reduce incoming sunlight as to bring on an ice age.

No one has yet provided a good reason for the earth's quirky magnetic behavior or even a fully satisfactory explanation to account for the magnetism in the first place. The best effort so far holds that the earth's molten outer core acts like a dynamo, or electrical generator, creating a magnetic field as it spins around the solid inner core. In any case, by 1963 a young British scientist, Frederick J. Vine, then 24 years old, had decided that changes in terrestrial magnetism could be used to test the sea-floor spreading hypothesis.

Vine pointed out that as lava oozed from the ridges and cooled, the rock would become indelibly imprinted with the earth's prevailing magnetic field. Even after the material had divided at the ridge and begun moving away from it in separate bands, it would retain this original magnetic signature. And like twins with the same genes, the polarity of the two stripes would always remain identical; no matter how far the stripes moved apart, those little magnets in the rock would point in the same direction. If there happened to be a subsequent magnetic flip-flop, it would leave its permanent stamp only on the warm emerging lava at the ridge, because once rock cools and hardens, its iron-bearing particles can no longer be easily realigned by an external magnetic force. Eventually, as more material oozed from the earth over geological time, repeated magnetic reversals would produce a whole series of zebralike stripes of alternating polarity running along the ridge.

Vine, who was still a graduate student at Cambridge University when he had his brainstorm, compared the emerging sea floor to recording tape. He said that it would faithfully record every switch of the earth's magnetic field as fresh sea floor reeled out of the ridges. Vine did not have to wait long for a playback. Only a year earlier, on an expedition to the Indian Ocean, his thesis adviser, Drummond H. Matthews, had found puzzling magnetic anomalies around the Carlsberg Ridge (named after the brewers of the Danish beer for their support of oceanographic research). Inspecting his professor's data, Vine spotted strong hints of magnetic striping parallel to the crustal divide. Still better evidence came from a detailed reconnaissance of a leg of the Mid-Atlantic Ridge off southern Iceland. There the magnetic maps showed zebralike stripes on opposite sides of the ridge that were virtually mirror images of one another. The symmetry was exactly what could be expected if the Hess-Dietz hypothesis were true.

There was an unfortunate sidelight to Vine's triumph. Even before he published his prediction in the British journal *Nature*, a Canadian scientist, Lawrence W. Morley, had conceived a similar theory. But his paper was rejected by leading scientific publications as too speculative and was not printed until the following year—in an obscure Canadian journal, where it was read by only a handful of scientists. Morley's distressing experience, which deprived him of proper credit for his equally original insight, indicated just how strong the opposition still was to the idea of drift.

But Vine soon weighed in with more evidence that helped erode the wall of skepticism. In collaboration with the Canadian geophysicist J. Tuzo Wilson, a fervent "drifter," he worked out actual speeds for the spreading. Their guidepost was a known chronology of the earth's magnetic reversals, worked out with land rocks by scientists of the U.S. Geological Survey's laboratories in Menlo Park, California, a major center of earthquake research. After testing the polarity of the rocks, the scientists had calibrated their ages by radioactive dating methods. Such "atomic clocks" depend on one of those miraculous phenomena by which nature sometimes reveals its secrets: the orderly decay, or breakdown, of radioactive elements into simpler, nonradioactive atoms. By measuring how much of this nuclear debris had accumulated in a particular rock—in this case, the gas argon, a by-product of radioactive potassium—the scientists could tell with reasonable accuracy how long ago the rock was formed.

Carefully matching their own magnetic patterns in the sea floor with the Menlo Park chronology, Vine and Wilson obtained ages for certain stripes. According to the spreading hypothesis, their ages would also represent the length of time it took the stripes to reach their current positions since they started inching away from the ridge. A three-million-year-old stripe, say, would have been moving for three million years. Assuming that Hess's conveyor belt operated roughly at a uniform rate, Vine and Wilson simply divided the stripe's present distance from its mid-ocean birthplace by its age to obtain its average speed during those travels. Around the East Pacific Rise, a ridge located in the Pacific Ocean off Central America and associated with the San Andreas fault, the typical rate of spreading turned out to be about two inches per year. Near Iceland it was only about a fourth of that speed. Nonetheless, the velocities were in accord with geological evidence that suggested the North Atlantic began to open up some 180 million years ago.

Wilson, perhaps the most eloquent advocate of the continental drift theory at the time, contributed other important evidence involving the mid-ocean ridges themselves. As more and more detailed maps of the sea floor became available, geologists realized that the ridges do not cleave the oceans in a straight line, but follow an irregular steplike pattern. At each "step," the ridge is displaced to one side or the other, sometimes by many hundreds of miles. These offsets are connected by long faults, which themselves often extend for hundreds of miles on both sides of the ridge. Geologists were at a loss to explain the fractures, or why the ridge was offset, except possibly as a sign that the ridge was pulling apart, like a crack in the shell of a cooked egg.

While fiddling with some paper models, Wilson suddenly saw in the puzzling faults a connection with sea-floor spreading. If the Hess-Dietz hypothesis were correct, he explained, the faults had to be an entirely new type of geological phenomenon, which he called transform faulting. As he saw it, the faults underwent a kind of a role reversal, or transformation of character, when they met the ridge. With his little paper models, he showed that unlike seemingly similar faults on land, the blocks on either side of the fracture were not sliding in opposite directions. Rather, because of sea-floor spreading, these chunks had to be moving away from the ridges in the same way. The only opposing motion, he demonstrated, came in the relatively small section of the fault connecting an offset.

The mid-ocean ridge system forms almost a continuous scar around globe. Inset shows close-up of transform fault, where only opposing motion occurs between ridge offsets. For this reason, most quakes along ridge occur in these regions.

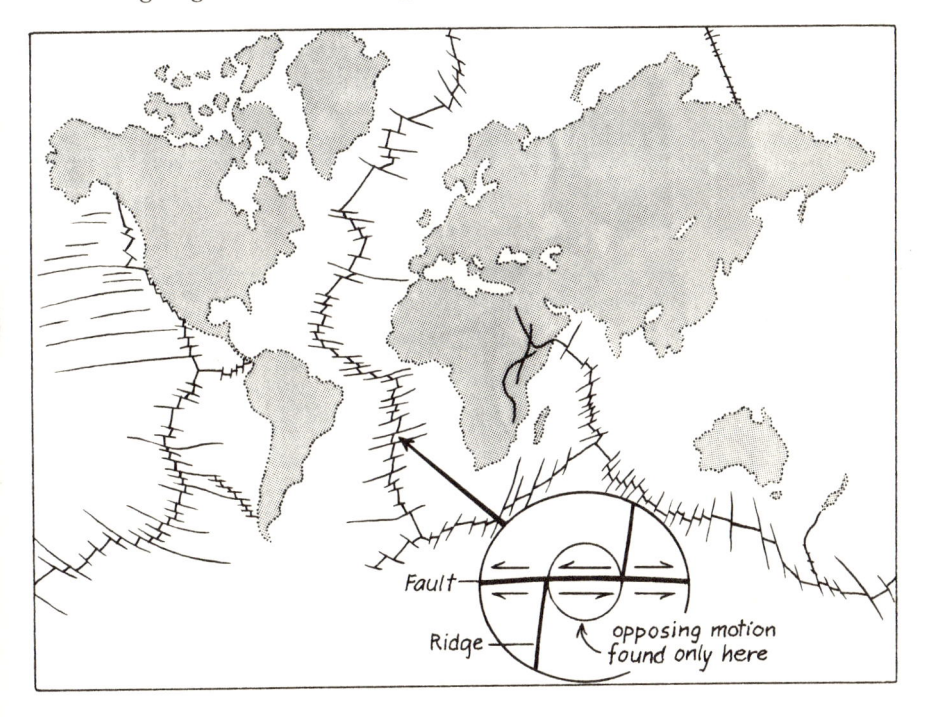

Wilson's models helped explain some curious seismic activity along the ridges. Like so many other discoveries of this era, this activity had come to light in an unexpected way. To detect and locate secret underground nuclear explosions, the United States had vastly improved its seismic capability during the Cold War years after World War II. In Montana alone, the Defense Department established an array of 525 interconnected seismometers, spread over an area as large as New Jersey. The region was chosen because its bedrock was considered especially responsive to seismic reverberations, like a finely cast bell. But the nuclear-blast detection machinery was also extremely valuable in the service of pure science. Its sensitive seismic ears could detect naturally occurring earthquakes virtually anywhere on (or under) the earth. As Berkeley's Bruce Bolt recalls, thanks to the Pentagon's generous support, "seismology was transformed from a neglected orphan of the physical sciences into a family favorite."

The new family favorite had its hands full. As data flooded in from their listening posts, seismologists started keeping global charts, like Robert Mallet's pioneering effort a century earlier. Every time a quake was picked up, they recorded its epicenter with a dot on their world maps. A pattern quickly emerged. Most of the shallow quakes were occurring along the mid-ocean ridges and most of the deep-focus ones near the deep-sea trenches, especially around the Ring of Fire. These areas were doing an incredible amount of shaking. As the dots piled up, they began to form thick lines, and it started to look as if the ridges and trenches were boundaries cutting up the earth's crust. To believers in sea-floor spreading, the results of the seismic mapping were not very surprising. If ocean floor is in fact being created at the ridges and being destroyed at the trenches, they would be constantly rumbling with quakes.

The Visionaries Prevail

But at least one detail of this seismicity remained a puzzle. It involved the quakes around Wilson's transform faults. As one of the overseers of the worldwide earthquake watch, Lamont-Doherty seismologist Lynn R. Sykes noticed that along most of their length the faults were seismically quiet. The only quakes he found were concentrated within the offsets, usually at the surface or only a few miles below it. Why should this be? On land, quakes can be expected to strike anywhere along a fault's length. After toying with his models, Wilson provided the answer. The quakes were bunching along this stretch because, under the sea-floor spreading hypothesis, it was the only part of the fault where the sea-floor was tugging in opposite directions. And so it would also be the only place along the fault rattled by quakes.

Wilson's paper models seemed to have provided a pretty convincing explanation of the earthquake data. But they did not constitute real proof; there might still be other ways of accounting for all the shaking within the offsets. What was needed were actual measurements showing opposing movements along these sections of the faults. But how could this be done under thousands of feet of water? Again it was the Pentagon's new sharp-eared seismic detectors that provided the answer. When an atomic bomb explodes underground, it pushes the rock out in all directions, so that a seismograph always registers an increase in pressure initially. By contrast, natural earthquakes push and pull the ground in opposite directions along a fault. This causes more complicated ground motions. If a seismograph happens to be located on the side of a fault away from the direction of movement, the instrument will probably first detect a falloff in pressure, while a detector on the other side records a rise. These differences not only let seismologists distinguish nuclear blasts from other, natural tremors. They can also tell them which way the ground is moving on either side of a fault.

Going back to his own records and those of other observatories, Sykes analyzed the patterns of 30 quakes along the mid-ocean ridges and the transform faults. In every case, the ground motion conformed exactly to Wilson's explanation. Within the offsets, the transform faults moved in opposite directions. Outside the offsets, the ground on each side of the faults moved in the same direction. In the ridges themselves, sea floor pushed upward and outward. These observations not only bore Wilson out but also supported the idea that new crustal material was welling up through the ridges. The Hess-Dietz hypothesis was looking better all the time.

By now Sykes himself was fast becoming converted to the idea of sea-floor spreading. "I really got steamed up," he recalls, and turned his talents to analyzing the earthquake activity at the other end of the oceanic conveyor belt. In some ways the quakes in the trenches were even more puzzling than those at the ridges. They were occurring far into the mantle at depths where the earth's rock was presumed to be so soft as to be fracture-proof. Again sea-floor spreading offered an explanation. As Dietz had noted, the ocean floor moves together with a layer of underlying mantle as a single, solid slab of lithosphere. This slab, or plate, travels unhindered until it runs into another plate coming from the opposite direction. The encounter is violent and catastrophic, with one plate crumpling over the other. As the lower plate presses down, it forms the V-shaped trench. Quakes rattle the earth along the entire length of the stormy encounter.

Sykes's seismographs soon gave him exceptionally good evidence of these crashes. He did his primary probing in the area of the Tonga trench, a deep crevasse in the South Pacific, off Samoa, not far from the site of the famed mutiny aboard *H.M.S. Bounty* in April 1789. Plotting the telltale quakes by both depth and position, rather than just on a surface map, Sykes obtained what was in effect a three-dimensional picture of the collision. Not only did the pattern of quakes show the direction of the plate's descent back into the earth (at a slope of about 45 degrees), but it actually provided an outline of the plate against the slightly different rock of the mantle. Captain Bligh, who was cast off by the mutineers in a small boat above this geophysical chaos, could hardly have known that an even more ferocious collision was taking place far below.

These seismic studies virtually clinched the case for sea-floor spreading, convincing even such recalcitrants as Maurice Ewing, who kept asking for more evidence. But a few scientists remained skeptical. Among of these nonbelievers was Vladimir V. Beloussov, the venerable dean of Soviet geologists. In one famous debate with Tuzo Wilson, he scornfully dismissed the sea floor's magnetic reversals as evidence. He complained that they were so confused an observer could see in them almost anything the imagination conjured up. "Remember the 'canals' on Mars!" warned Beloussov, recalling a famous example of misidentification by the turn-of-the-century astronomer Percival Lowell. While viewing the dusty surface of Mars through his telescope, Lowell became convinced he saw intricate irrigation networks and offered them as proof of intelligent life on the red planet. Close-up probes of Mars have now shown that Lowell's canals could be nothing more than shifting sands, blown by the red planet's high winds.

To old-guard geologists like Beloussov, reams of computer paper filled with magnetic or seismic data would never do. Before they accepted the new ideas, they wanted the kind of evidence they could feel in their hands, chip with their hammers, and subject to close-up scrutiny. In a word, they wanted rocks. But collecting specimens from the bottom of the sea is no simple matter. The average depth of the oceans is more than two miles. A drill "string" long enough to reach all the way down would weigh many tons. If the ship suddenly lurched in wind or waves, the rig might snap and thousands of dollars' worth of equipment would sink to the bottom.

In 1968 a remarkable vessel especially built for the difficult task set out to begin sampling the deep-sea floor. It was the 400-foot, 10,500-ton drill ship *Glomar Challenger*, named after her owners, Global Marine Inc., and the pioneering British oceanographic vessel *Challenger*, which made a memorable three-and-a-half-year-long survey of the seas in the 1870s. During her first five years of operation, *Glomar Challenger* retrieved samples from all the oceans except the Arctic.

Looking like a floating oil derrick, she lowered her five-inch-diameter drill pipes in 90-foot lengths through a well in the center of the ship. Guided by navigational satellites, she maintained position over a hole by computer-controlled thrusters on opposite sides of the hull. She drilled in depths of almost four miles and, at times, pulled up pipefuls of sediment and rock totaling nearly a mile in length. From the fossilized microorganisms in the samples, called cores, the scientists could obtain a good estimate of the sediment's age. In a few cases, *Glomar Challenger*'s drilling apparatus reached the volcanic bedrock underlying the sea-bottom sediment, presumably part of the original ocean floor created at the ridges.

But the Deep Sea Drilling Project, as it was called, was more than a technological triumph. As *Glomar Challenger* drilled farther from the ridges, the samples of ocean floor became progressively older and the carpet of sediment was found to be thicker. These results were a stunning affirmation of sea-floor spreading and continental drift. The ages of the cores also provided a drift chronology. North America probably broke from Africa 135 million years ago. The two Americas became joined

The Visionaries Prevail

about 65 million years ago. India crashed into Asia 40 million years ago, creating the Himalayas in the collision and leaving China crisscrossed with faults that still rock that nation today. Even skeptics had to heed the message from the deep. While rocks forged nearly 4 billion years ago have been uncovered on dry land, nothing older than 160 million years—barely 5 percent of the age of the earth—turned up on the sea floor. As Hess had said, it is the ocean basins that are young and forever changing.

With *Glomar Challenger* bringing back more and more evidence, there was no stopping the revolution in geological thinking. No longer were scientists talking only of ridges and trenches, of magnetic anomalies and transform faults. They began to see the whole planet in a sharp new light. Sea-floor spreading became plate tectonics. The earth's outer shell was, in a sense, not a shell at all; it consisted of a half dozen major plates and a number of minor ones. The United States rode on the North American plate, sharing it with Canada, Mexico, and half the Atlantic. The Pacific had a plate all to itself. There were also Africian, Eurasian, South American, Australian, and Antarctic plates, each of them bearing a slice of the continental pie.

The plates were in a permanent frenzy, bumping and crunching, destroying old rocks and making new ones. But on a human scale, there was barely any action at all. The Atlantic was expanding at a rate of two inches a year, parts of the Pacific were contracting by four. Half a lifetime might pass before an ocean grew or shrank the length of the human body. But in time, over geology's eras and epochs, the inches would become miles. New oceans would emerge, old ones would die. The continents would move, wandering like refugees in search of new homes. And some might even slowly split apart.

The dance of the continents has gone on for a very long time. Wegener spoke of Pangaea as the primordial landmass. But even it seems to have had ancestors. Recently some scientists have concluded that the continents have been breaking apart and coming together for billions for years. One such episode may have started 450 million years ago when an earlier Atlantic began to close and uplifted the Appalachian mountains of the eastern United States. Still other newly discovered signs of early drift are fragments on the ocean floor of what appear to be long lost continents.

And the continents will continue their meanderings in the future. Cranking known rates of drift into a computer, Dietz and a colleague, John C. Holden, have looked ahead 50 million years, at an earth that is a world far different from ours. Australia, after drifting north, is now rubbing against the Asian mainland. The Americas have broken apart, but new land has been uplifted out of the Caribbean. East Africa has split from the rest of the continent, while the sliver of California west of the San Andreas fault is abreast of Canada. Almost before geologists can say Lower Cretaceous, Los Angeles will be ready to slide into the Aleutian trench.

The crystal ball may be an amusing plaything for the wizards of the new geology. But the real significance of plate tectonics is how it can be applied here and now. Oil and mineral hunters are already using the theory to lead them to new underground treasure. A rich lode in one geological formation could lead to similar treasure in related terrain that now sits a drifted-continent away. The mountains of copper and tin in South America, for example, may be estranged cousins of what could turn out to be ore-rich hills in Antarctica. Yet the biggest payoff from plate tectonics could come from something that has nothing to do with the earth's hidden wealth.

Since the theory unfolded, scientists have used it to explain many of geology's old puzzles. Mountains are built where the

The Visionaries Prevail

plates crash head on. Where they slide under each other, they lift island arcs like the Japanese archipelago and forge volcanoes. Where they tear apart, they create new ocean floor, more volcanoes, and snippets of land like Iceland. And wherever their paths cross, they cause earthquakes.

The San Andreas fault is the place where the North American plate meets up with the Pacific. As the plates try to slide past each other, parts of them inevitably stick, rapidly building up strain in the bedrock. If they remain stuck too long, the result will be a quake like San Francisco's 1906 jolt. For the moment, scientists can do nothing to avert such a calamity. There is no way to prevent a major quake, yet. But comprehending nature is usually the first step to coping with it. Spurred by the advances in seismology, scientists have been making promising advances in earthquake prediction. The broader understanding of quakes that has come from plate tectonics may lead to the realization of another dream: the day when it will be possible to control the earth's ugly rampages.

8 seismologists who ARE SEERS

To the farmers and shepherds of the Pamir Mountains, just across the border from Afghanistan in the Soviet Central Asian republic of Tadzhikistan, there is nothing unusual about earthquakes. They are so commonplace that the inhabitants of this wildly beautiful terrain barely pause in their daily chores when walls shake and windows rattle. In July 1949, after a quake was felt in the town of Khait, at the base of a narrow, isolated valley in Tadzhikistan's Garm District, only a few people noticed that a huge chunk of land was missing from one of the steep hills overlooking the community. The earth's tremors had shaken loose tons of rock and dirt. But the people just shrugged fatalistically and went about their business. Quakes were God's will, they realized. Nothing could be done about them.

If they had looked closer they would have seen a disturbing sight. High up in the hills, out of the view of the town, the avalanche had formed a natural earthen dam across the valley. Rapidly collecting behind the fragile barrier were streams of water coming down from the mountains. A day or two after the quake, the dam burst, bringing almost instant destruction to the town. Within moments Khait lay buried under 100 feet of mud and rock. Only a handful of the 12,000 townspeople escaped with their lives.

The disaster had reverberations as far away as Moscow. Coming as it did, only ten months after a quake claimed 20,000 lives in the Soviet Central Asian city of Ashkhabad 700 miles to the west, the dam's collapse made the Kremlin resolve to avoid such tragedies in the future. A major seismological task force was organized and sent off to the remote mountain region. Its assignment was to find a way of predicting when and where a quake would strike. Nature, the Soviets were sure, must provide some clues before the ground's catastrophic rupture. Once these precursors were identified, they could perhaps be used as early-warning signals for earthquakes.

The undertaking carried the government's highest priority. Scientists were scattered across the Garm District with their families and settled into remote houses in seismically active areas. Each of these dwellings came with a clutch of instruments, including seismographs, which the scientists were responsible for monitoring and maintaining. Once a week a truck came by with food and supplies and to pick up the record of the earth's tremblings during the previous seven days. The network of stations was primitive by today's standards, but it enabled the Soviet scientists to keep track of every twitch of the earth in the tremulous regions.

As the months and years passed, the data from the little observatories grew into a mountain of measurements. But nature did not seem very willing to tip its hand. As hard as they tried, the Soviet scientists could not find anything in the seismic record that provided the slightest hint of an imminent quake. Apparently it was not enough just to record the area's background seismic noise—the almost imperceptible micro tremors that nearly always seemed to be shaking the needles of Garm's seismographs. The earth had to be providing the clues in some other way. Unwilling to give up their search, the determined Soviet investigators resorted to new strategies. They kept watch on the tilt of the land, observed the level of water in wells, and took readings of the local magnetic fields. Rigging four miles of wire across one stretch of the quake-riddled district, they even checked for changes in the electrical conductivity of crustal rock. All these efforts had a single aim. It was to find some sign of the earth's growing anger before it actually erupted.

Because of language and political barriers, hardly anyone in the West knew of the intensive Soviet efforts to learn the secrets of quake forecasting. But in 1971, at an international earthquake conference hosted by the Russians in Moscow, they finally gave a detailed report on their work. Astonished Western scientists learned that the Soviet researchers had apparently made a major breakthrough in quake prediction. Though the Russians initially saw nothing unusual in the earth's ever-present vibrations, on closer inspection, they found that their seismograms showed a curious change in wave behavior just before three different quakes. By using this clue as a sign of a quake's imminence, the Soviets told the Moscow meeting, they had been able to anticipate several subsequent tremors.

At the time the exact nature of the change was not known even to the Soviets. But it centered on the relative velocities of the two basic types of seismic waves: P or primary waves and S or secondary waves. As already noted, primary waves reach seismic stations first because they travel faster than secondary waves through the earth's bedrock. Typically, the ratio of their velocities is about 1.75 to 1. However, in the weeks or months before the three quakes, the gap between the two types of waves had inexplicably closed. For a time, the waves were arriving much closer together. Then the interval suddenly returned to normal.

When that happened, the quake soon followed. The Soviets had no idea whether the P waves had slowed down, or whether the S waves had sped up, or whether both had occurred. But one thing was apparent: the same velocity changes showed up in the records before all three quakes. It was clear to the careful Russian scientists that their observations were no fluke. In each case, the change in the relative velocities of the P and S waves was about 6 percent. At last the Soviets appeared to have found their long elusive prequake signal.

In their studies, they also made another important discovery: the longer the abnormal velocities lasted, the greater the quake was likely to be. Prior to the largest quake, for example, the change in arrival times of the P and S waves continued for three months; before the middle-sized quake, about a month and a half; and before the smallest quake, only 34 days. This meant that the Soviets could not only forecast a quake but anticipate its magnitude as well.

Why were the Russians the first to spot the abnormal wave behavior rather than any scientists in the United States or Japan, where intensive investigations into earthquakes had also been going on for a long time? The question is all the more intriguing in light of the availability in these countries of much more sophisticated instruments to monitor fault zones. Ironically, say some American seismologists, the answer may lie in the very primitiveness of the Soviet effort. Lacking computers to sift through and analyze their store of data, the Russian scientists were forced to process it manually, painstakingly plotting out such things as the arrival of different seismic waves on charts and blackboards. In this way, the subtle velocity shifts obscured in the mass of readings became graphically visible.

As soon as he returned home from Moscow, Lamont-Doherty's Lynn Sykes urged one of his graduate students, an Indian doctoral candidate in seismology named Yash Aggarwal, to put the Russian claims to the test. The Columbia researchers had just the place for such an experiment. For a number of years, they had been operating a network of seismographs in the Blue Mountain Lake region of the Adirondack Mountains in upper New York State. Frequently shaken by tiny tremors, it is an ideal laboratory for seismological studies. Combing through the records of the area's past seismic activity, Aggarwal noticed that a series of small quakes, or what seismologists call a swarm, had occurred at just about the time of the Moscow conference. Before each of the quakes, Aggarwal discovered, there had been a temporary yet distinct closing of the gap in the arrival of the P and S waves.

Across the country at Caltech, seismologists also started rummaging through their records to look for velocity changes. Examining seismograms of the earth's movements before the 1971 San Fernando Valley quake, James Whitcomb, John Garmany, and Don Anderson produced what they believed was in effect a retrospective prediction of that powerful shock. They saw that there had been a distinct drop-off in the velocity of the P waves (rather than a speedup of the S waves) starting as long as three and a half years before the jolt. The extended period seemed to be vivid proof of the Soviet contention that the duration of the abnormality was also a sign of the impending quake's size.

Besides verifying the Soviet report, Whitcomb and his colleagues showed that the new prediction technique might work even in the absence of the sort of background seismic noise that regularly shakes Garm or the Adirondacks. All that would be needed in these relatively quiet (but hardly earthquake-free) zones are some artificially created waves. As it happens, explosives trigger the crucial P waves much more readily than S waves. The California work also demonstrated that the P-wave velocity changes were not a quirk of the local geology in Garm or the Adirondacks but a broader phenomenon, perhaps characteristic of quake activity in widely different parts of the world.

Until these startling developments, attempts to forecast earthquakes had been almost exclusively the province of assorted psychics, mystics, astrologers, and charlatans. This soothsaying tradition dates at least as far back as the Romans, who did not hesitate to consult their priests and oracles about the imminence of such natural calamities as earthquakes. Even in our scientific age, there is no shortage of people who claim the special gift to foretell quakes, volcanic eruptions, and other terrestrial disasters. These prophets of gloom and doom make so many predictions that occasionally one of the forecasts appears to hit the mark, thereby ensuring the reputations of those who advance them among the gullible. But seismologists are not content with prophecies conjured out of thin air or lively imaginations. To be scientific, a quake prediction must be based on some substantive evidence of the earth's internal unrest, preferably a physical clue from the ground itself. Also, it must specify the range of the earthquake's magnitude, the area where it will strike, and the time of that occurrence, along with some calculation of the odds that the prediction will come true. These are strict criteria, rarely met by the self-styled earthquake seers. With the Russian precursors, seismologists finally had the means to try making forecasts in such a scientifically acceptable way.

No one understood the underlying mechanism at work in the prequake velocity changes, although this much was plain about them: whatever it was that was affecting the speed of the seismic waves, it had to have something to do with the material they were traveling through—the earth's bedrock. Late in the nineteenth century, a British-Irish physicist named Osborne Reynolds showed that when granular substances like rock are subjected to stress, they swell or expand. He called the phenomenon dilatancy, from the verb "dilate," or spread apart. Osborne's research was largely ignored by the scientific community until the 1960s. Then a geologist at the Massachusetts Institute of Technology, William F. Brace, began studying the behavior of rock while it was being put under enormous pressure. Brace and his young colleagues discovered that as the material comes close to the breaking point, it develops countless microscopic cracks, almost like the pores in skin. By adding to the rock's volume, these tiny "pores" brought about the expansion observed by Reynolds in his tests more than half a century earlier.

Dilatancy also caused other effects. The M.I.T. investigators showed that it reduced the ability of the rock to conduct electricity and slowed the speed of sound waves passing through it. Brace himself suggested that these physical changes might somehow be used to forecast earthquakes, but at the time he had no idea how to put his farsighted proposal to work. Dilatancy was obviously an interesting example of the behavior of materials under stress, yet it remained little more than a laboratory curiosity until the Russians reported their prequake observations, followed by the swift confirmation of their work in the United States. Almost immediately, two of Brace's former students, Amos Nur and Christopher Scholz, realized that there was a connection between their old experiments at M.I.T. and the new seismic findings. That link was dilatancy.

By then the Israeli-born Nur was a geophysicist at Stanford University and Scholz had become a colleague of Sykes's at Lamont-Doherty. In separate but almost simultaneously published papers, they explored how dilatancy would affect the properties of rock before a quake. They pointed out that as the material comes under increasing strain, it develops cracks

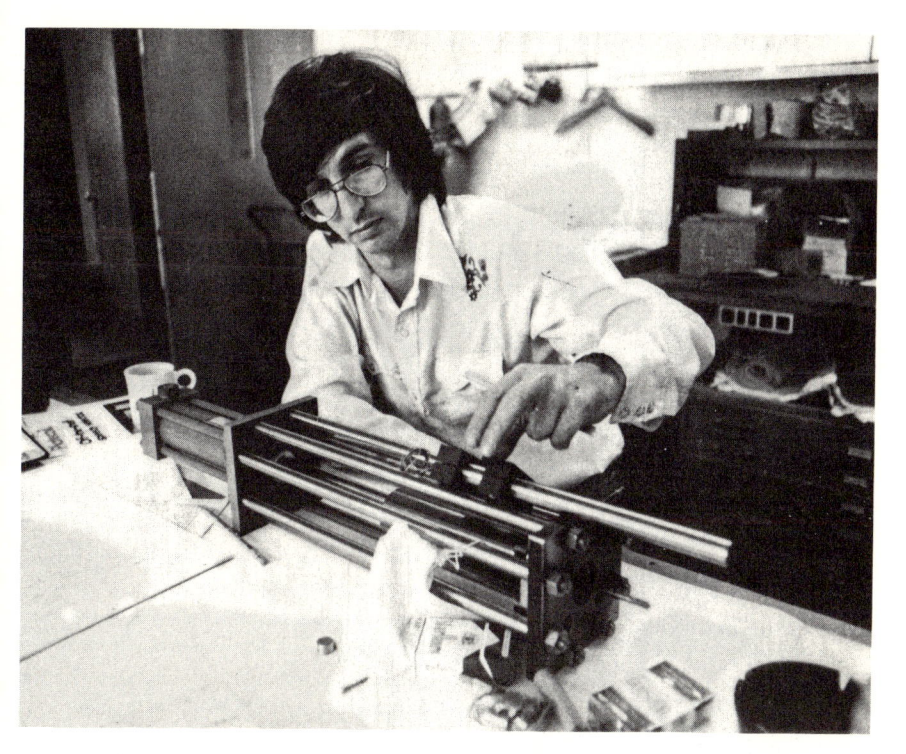

Geologist Christopher H. Scholz, who helped explain the dilatancy theory of quake prediction, forces water through rock in an experiment in his laboratory at Lamont-Doherty.

throughout and swells in size. The fissuring also lowers the pressure of any water that may have been in the rock's existing voids. This strengthens the rock and perhaps explains why there is a sharp decline in minor shaking just before a large quake. The slowdown in the seismic waves is the result of the tiny fissures as well. The fissures make the rock less rigid and more elastic, and as Mallet had shown long ago (see Chapter 4), that retards the passage of any waves through it. But eventually groundwater seeps into the pores, and because P waves travel almost as quickly through water as they do through the rock itself, their velocity picks up again and returns to normal. At the same time the water tends to weaken the rock until it finally gives and the quake occurs.

An example of such water-induced quaking had just recently been observed in the United States. In 1965 a Denver geologist, David M. Evans, pointed out that small earthquakes had been rattling the usually tremor-free Denver area ever since the U.S. army began disposing of poisonous wastes from its nerve-gas manufacturing facilities at the nearby Rocky Mountain Arsenal. Ironically, the army thought it was getting rid of the lethal chemicals in an absolutely safe manner. It was pumping them under high pressure into two-mile deep fractures in the bedrock. These cracks had been created by underground blasting at the bottom of a well specifically drilled to keep deadly wastes away from drinking water supplies. Only when the army stopped injecting the fluids into the earth did the tremors ease. Seismologists suggested that the quaking could be shut off entirely if the chemicals were pumped out. Aside from the immediate practical benefit, they had a scientific reason for making the proposal. Such a test would demonstrate for the first time that quakes could be brought under control at will. Officials, however, refused to let the scientists tamper with the underground fluids for fear of setting off even larger quakes.

There was cause for concern. The construction of large dams holding back huge reservoirs had already indicated that quakes can be triggered accidentally when water seeps into subterranean rock. Following completion of the 726-foot-high Hoover Dam in 1935, when the Colorado River began to create Lake Mead, small earthquakes started shaking the Arizona-Nevada border area. Some were strong enough to rattle the gaming tables of nearby Las Vegas. In 1962, after experiencing many thousands of tiny tremors, China's proud new Hsinfengkiang

Dam, north of Canton, was hit by a magnitude 6.1 earthquake. It severely damaged the 350-foot-high concrete structure. The strongest tremor linked to a dam occurred in 1967, when 177 people were killed and more than 1,500 injured by a powerful 6.5 jolt in Koyna, India. Presumably, in every one of these cases, water either weakened the rock under the reservoirs to the point of breaking or provided the "lubrication" that allowed previously undetected faults at the dam site to release.

In their explanation of the quake precursors that they had discovered, the Soviets deny that the strength of the rock is affected by the flow of water in and out of the pores. Rather, they say, it is simply the opening and closing of the tiny fissures prior to a quake that accounts for the changes in the wave velocities. However that may be, the Soviets themselves recorded an increase in local tremors when they finished their 1,000-foot-high Nurek Dam in Tadzhikistan, the highest earth-fill dam in the world.

A few years after the Denver tremors, scientists finally got a chance to try their hand at quake-taming. At the edge of its Rangely oil field in northwestern Colorado, the Chevron Oil Company had been pumping water under great pressure into "dry" wells so as to force every possible drop of petroleum out of the ground. Small tremors occurred during these operations, but no one could connect them definitely with injection of the water. In 1972, after setting up their instruments around the oil field, the scientists themselves began pumping water into four Chevron wells. The needles of their seismographs quickly responded by registering many tiny quakes. These tremors continued until the following March, when the water was at last removed. In a limited way, the experiment proved that it was possible to control earthquakes.

Encouraged by the success at Rangely, two U.S. Geological Survey scientists, C. Barry Raleigh (who subsequently became

Lamont-Doherty's director) and James Dietrich, stepped forward with a daring proposal. They suggested drilling a row of three deep holes about 500 yards apart along a section of a fault where stresses were building to the danger point. First they would pump out any water in the two outer holes, thus strengthening the rock surrounding them. Next they would inject water into the middle hole until the rock immediately around it failed. The result would be a minor quake. It would be contained between the locked areas and release the strain along this part of the fault. In theory at least, the technique could be used on a much grander scale, perhaps even to control the movements of faults as long as the San Andreas.

For such a huge undertaking, Raleigh explained, it might be necessary to drill some 500 holes as deep as three miles each. They would be evenly spaced along various quake-prone sections of the San Andreas where the earth's opposing tectonic plates had jammed. Then, by setting off one small quake after another up and down the fault with the three-hole technique, the strain could be progressively relieved along the entire length of the San Andreas. The plates would be allowed to continue on their way and a major quake would be averted. The authors of the proposal admit that, at least for now, it is an exercise in seismic science fiction. Carrying it out would cost billions of dollars and perhaps unleash a large tremor accidentally. But if the procedure succeeded in sparing California from the calamitous earthquake that all seismologists say will eventually come, it might someday be worth both the cost and the risk.

At the Moscow meeting, the Soviets had also reported changes in the electrical conductivity of the ground before a quake. Though they did not know what to make of these observations at the time of their discovery, they used them to predict a quake on Siberia's Kamchatka Peninsula. Off the USSR's Pacific coast across from Alaska, it is the site of frequent temblors and volcanic eruptions. According to the dilatancy theory, the explanation for the fluctuations in conductivity was simple: as the rock's pores open, its ability to conduct electricity goes down because air acts as an insulator and resists the flow of a current. Then as water seeps into the pores, conductivity rises because the liquid is a good conductor of electricity. The electrical changes may also be at the root of the variations in strength of local magnetic fields observed by the Soviets before some quakes. But some scientists have another explanation. They attribute changes in this natural magnetism to prequake stresses that distort the rock's internal, latticelike crystalline structure.

The dilatancy theory also seemed to explain why the Russians, as well as earthquake teams in China, had found increased levels of the radioactive gas radon in deep wells before some quakes. The Russians made the discovery serendipitously while they were routinely checking the chemical contents of hot springs near the ancient Central Asian city of Tashkent, north of the Pamir Mountains. Still, they did not recognize its importance right away. Shortly thereafter, on April 26, 1966, Tashkent was hit by a major quake that destroyed many historic buildings but fortunately took only a few lives. Again it was the tiny cracks in the rocks that appeared to hold the key to the radon in the wells. As the fissures spread, the rock exposes increased surface area to the surrounding material, enabling it to soak up, spongelike, more of the natural radioactive substances in the ground, including radon, a short-lived by-product of uranium. Then as water invades the pores, the radon is flushed out and it turns up in the wells.

The increase in the rock's volume also seemed to be at least partly responsible for the lifting and tilting of land that often takes place before quakes. Japanese seismologists had already observed this peculiarity in their effort to develop means of forecasting quakes on their tremor-wracked islands. As long as five years before a quake devastated the city of Niigata in 1964, they noticed that the ground there was starting to rise. The uplift reached a maximum of two inches, then it abruptly subsided. Misinterpreting the sign, the Japanese blamed the ground movements on the pumping of natural gas from a nearby field. The quake soon followed. However, the Japanese scientists redeemed themselves a year later when they used similar shifts of the ground to warn of impending quakes in the town of Matsushiro. The tremors began in 1965 and continued on and off for more than two years. During this period, houses creaked and swayed so often that many townspeople took to sleeping outdoors in their fields.

Heeding the Japanese experience, American scientists have been closely watching an area of crustal uplift along the San Andreas fault centered on the community of Palmdale, California, just 35 miles north of downtown Los Angeles at the edge of the Mojave Desert. The rise began in the 1960s and reached a maximum of about 20 inches by the mid-1970s, when sections of the area rapidly subsided, like a tire losing air. At least one scientist insisted that the measurements of an uplift were nothing more than a surveying error. But most scientists regarded the Palmdale Bulge, as it became known in newspaper headlines, as real enough, and it continued to be a cause for jitters in Southern California.

The dilatancy theory seemed to explain many quake omens. But some of the ground's writhings continued to puzzle scientists. Many seismologists doubt that fissuring alone could, for example, expand rock sufficiently to cause uplift on so large a scale as the Palmdale Bulge. A more plausible explanation may be that the land is being squeezed up directly, like a rug crumpled against a wall, by pressures accumulating along the San Andreas fault. Also, many quakes occur without any obvious precursors at all. Possibly, mechanisms of rock behavior other than dilatancy may predominate in certain seismic zones, especially those deep in the ground where no water is available to enter the rock. Nonetheless, as a theory of earthquake prediction, dilatancy seemed to be an impressive tool, perhaps of use in earthquake zones outside of the Soviet Union. Inspired by the Russian example, few American scientists could resist the temptation of trying to make some forecasts of their own.

They were surprisingly successful. In 1973, after poring over freshly collected tracings from Lamont-Doherty's seven portable seismographs in the Blue Mountain Lake area, Yash Aggarwal breathlessly called Sykes at the observatory. The P-wave velocities, he reported, indicated that a modest quake, perhaps magnitude 2.5 or 3, might occur at any moment. Two days later, as Aggarwal sat down to dinner at his rustic camp, he sensed the ground rumbling under him. "I could feel the waves passing," he recalled, "and I was jubilant." So jubilant was he, in fact, that he almost drove his truck into a tree on the way home. Aggarwal's quake was not much of a tremor, but it went down in the annals of seismology as the first to be scientifically predicted in the United States.

Only a few months later, Caltech's Whitcomb weighed in with his own triumph. In November, after spotting a sharp upswing in the velocity of P waves following a slowdown lasting more than a year, he flatly announced that a moderate quake would hit Riverside, California, within the next three months. The tremor came almost right on cue, although it was slightly weaker than predicted. On January 30, a magnitude 4.1 jolt hit the Riverside area. Whitcomb's quake was not only timely, it was well placed. Until then successful forecasts had always involved so-called thrust faults, where one block of rock is pushing directly against another. The Riverside quake occurred along a strike-slip fault, where two sections of rock are trying to slip by each other. That meant seismologists might well be able to use their new crystal ball to predict the violence of America's most notorious seismic divide, the San Andreas fault, whose general movements provide a textbook example of strike-slip faulting.

It was not long before the San Andreas gave seismologists just such an opportunity. The test case involved the town of Hollister, California, about 100 miles south of San Francisco. Slow fault movements, or what scientists call creep, along with small tremors, are such a regular part of life in Hollister that residents half-humorously have nicknamed it "The Earthquake Capital of the World." (Even so, Hollister has never been hit by a really damaging quake, perhaps because strain is being relieved by creep and other minor seismic activity.) Just a few miles out of town, the San Andreas cuts right under a winery, slowly tearing walls, floors, and foundations apart. The ground moves at an average rate of half an inch or so a year. Hollister itself sits directly atop a branch of the San Andreas called the Calaveras fault. Its creeping movements can be seen in offset streets and sidewalks, breaks in fences, and houses that are tilted and twisted. Making the most of Hollister's troublesome terrain, scientists have rigged the area with field instruments of every kind—strain gauges to measure the deformation of rock, tiltmeters to check ground levels, geodolites to track fault movements, and magnetometers to assess local magnetic fields, plus the usual array of seismometers. Most of this information is automatically sent by telephone lines and microwaves to the Geological Survey's Earthquake Prediction Center in Menlo Park.

In November 1974, while routinely examining data gathered during the preceding year, Malcolm Johnston, one of the center's seismologists, came upon some worrisome signs. He noticed that the strength of the local magnetic field had recently risen between two stations over a period of about a week. Then suddenly it had gone down. Simultaneously, other instruments had picked up a slight shift in the ground's tilt. Discussing these changes with his fellow earth scientists at an informal monthly meeting of California's Pick and Hammer Club, Johnston said that they were just "the sort one would expect to see before a quake." Another Geological Survey scientist, John Healy, was even more emphatic. He warned that Hollister could soon expect a quake of magnitude 5 on the Richter scale. And when would it take place? he was asked. "Maybe tomorrow," he replied. The next afternoon, November 28, 1974, while many residents of Hollister were sitting down to their Thanksgiving Day dinners, the ground shook briefly but powerfully. Hollister had been hit by a magnitude 5.2 quake.

The tremor lasted only a second or two and did no real damage, but it showed how useful the precursors might be for quake forecasting. Indeed, by then scientists had evolved a whole set of guidelines to interpret the warnings. If changes in P-wave velocities, say, or magnetic fields were detected over a wide area, the quake would be extremely powerful but might not occur for months or even years. On the other hand, if the changes were limited to a small area, the earthly disturbance would be weak but probably take place soon. In either case, the quake's timing could be approximately determined. Once the abnormalities had vanished, the quake usually followed after a period about a tenth as long as the duration of the observed precursors. Thus, if the abnormalities suddenly stopped registering on instruments after ten months, a quake could be expected about a month later. By this rule of thumb, the warning signs of an extremely powerful event like Alaska's 1964 Good Friday earthquake should begin to appear as long as 40 years before its occurrence. Unfortunately, seismologists do not yet have seismic records of sufficient accuracy that go far enough back to forecast such blockbuster quakes. Nor is it certain, even if such records existed, that they would show clearcut signs of velocity changes or other precursors.

But the earth's history may in fact offer clues to the coming of a big quake. In the mid-1960s a Soviet seismologist named S. A. Fedotov began mapping the sites and the extent of large quakes that had hit northern Japan since 1904. He began to notice a pattern: the quakes seemed to have taken place in a row, one after another, like a string of firecrackers popping. Usually quakes recurred in any given area at a frequency of about once every 30 years. Following his quake line north, he noticed an ominous sign: the Kurile Islands, just south of the Kamchatka Peninsula, had been seismically quiet far too long. Quakes were seriously overdue. And soon Fedotov's scientific premonition came true. Within the next few years, the Kuriles were rocked by four large temblors.

Regions marked by foreboding lulls in earthquake activity are called seismic gaps. They are usually located along active plate boundaries, where the earth's giant crustal blocks are pushing past or pressing under each other. The long absence of major quakes in any particular area may simply mean that the buildup of strain is being relieved by creep or small quakes. This lets the plates move along relatively smoothly. But a gap can also be a warning sign, an indication that the plates are locked. The strain may be building to intolerable levels in the gap zone. The accumulating forces eventually must be released in a giant quake.

Seismologists Who Are Seers

In 1968, after spotting a gap in the Alaska panhandle, Lynn Sykes forecast a magnitude 7.5 quake in the area of Sitka, the old Russian territorial capital. Four years later the region was hit by a 7.6 quake. In 1979 Sykes, along with his colleagues Klaus Jacob, William McCann, and Omar Perez, identified another alarming gap near Cape Yakataga along the southern coast of Alaska, about 230 miles east of Anchorage. What caught their eyes was the fact that major quakes had recently occurred to the east and west, but there had been no quake of comparable size within the gap since 1899. All the while the Pacific plate has presumably been thrusting northward under the North American plate at a rate of two or more inches a year, enormously increasing strains along this jammed section. Like much of Alaska, the area is largely uninhabited except for the tiny village of Yakataga (population: about ten). The Columbia scientists said that the region would be the setting of a "great earthquake" (magnitude 8 or higher) anytime within the next few decades.

Since the emergence of the gap concept, scientists at Columbia and elsewhere have been plotting worldwide maps showing where earthquakes have occurred and where they are overdue. The charts reveal at least two dozen gaps, most of them along the Pacific's Ring of Fire. Intriguingly, some gaps are bracketed on either side by the sites of recent smaller quakes, usually registering no more than about magnitude 6 or 7. These events could well be foreshocks of the great quake to come. On the charts, they form oval-shaped patterns around the gaps. Because of their configuration, they have been dubbed Mogi's doughnuts, after their discoverer, the Japanese seismologist Kiyo Mogi. By taking into account the size and the seismic history of the gaps, the Columbia seismologists have even been able to rank them on a scale indicating a quake's likelihood. The values range from one to six, with the odds for a quake rising as the numbers go down. Placed in the number one, or highest risk, category are gaps off the Shumagin Islands in Alaska, in the Caribbean near Puerto Rico, and off the Indonesian island of Sumatra.

The most dramatic application of the gap theory came with the successful prediction of an earthquake in the southern Mexican state of Oaxaca in 1978. By then scientists had learned there is a certain preliminary pattern. The gaps enter a period of seismic quiet, during which there is hardly a shake of the ground, followed by swarms of small tremors. In 1977, after noting the extreme inactivity of a section of the Mexican coast where the Pacific plate is pressing under North America, scientists at the Geophysics Laboratory of the University of Texas at Galveston concluded that it was a gap in its early, quiescent phase. The seismologists, Tosimatu Matumoto, Gary Latham, and Masakazu Ohtake, forecast a quake up to magnitude 7.75 but could not pin down when exactly it might occur.

During the following summer, Karen McNally, then a senior research fellow in seismology from Caltech, was visiting the Institute of Geophysics in Mexico City. Suddenly, alarm bells sounded in the institute's basement, where its seismographs are kept. The jiggling needles were registering the second series of moderate tremors in the Oaxaca area in five weeks. McNally, who specialized in the study of micro tremors, knew of the Texas seismologists' prediction and realized that the Oaxaca shaking could be the forerunner of a major quake. She persuaded the Mexican government to let her set up a network of seven portable seismographs in the wilds of Oaxaca. Her objective was to catch the big quake in the making, especially the weak foreshocks that only register on seismographs when they are placed almost atop the shaking ground. Such measurements, she realized, could do much to hone seismology's skills at forecasting.

Seismologist Karen McNally, who recorded a big quake during its birth pangs, explains a point while studying enlargements of a seismogram on microfilm projector.

By November the instruments were in place and McNally was ready. After a week, the seismographs resonated to a series of small tremors, only magnitude 3.2. Then there was another quiet spell. On November 28 the ground was shaken by a second series of small quakes. This time they were a little larger, magnitude 3.7. Eighteen hours later, as the early afternoon sun blazed overhead, the major quake came. Its violent motions rocked the earth, to say nothing of McNally's instruments. Though no one was injured along the sparsely settled coast, the big temblor, about magnitude 7.5 to 7.8, shook buildings and cracked walls in Mexico City, nearly 300 miles away.

McNally had succeeded gloriously in her mission. Every pulse of the earth—from the first hints of ground movement to the final big jolts—was recorded by her array, which had been planted almost in the heart of the rumblings. Her measurements were a seismological first. Never before had instruments captured the full unraveling of a major quake. From these invaluable data, as well as recordings of other foreshocks that might be made by other alert scientists in the future, there could emerge reliable guidelines telling seismologists almost exactly when gaps seem ready to give.

Yet all gaps are not alike, and different rules may apply for each. In places where one plate is thrusting under another, as along the coast of Oaxaca, gaps may display all the prequake unrest recorded by Karen McNally's seismographs. But when plates slide past each other, or do a little of both—thrusting and sliding—as in Southern California, their behavior becomes harder to fathom. Many scientists believe that Southern California shows classic gap symptoms, but others feel that the methods used to forecast the Oaxaca quake are not applicable to this part of the San Andreas. Even so, there is no argument between the two schools over one geophysical fact: in the Los Angeles area, the plates appear tightly locked. No major earthquake has moved them since the morning of September 9, 1857, when the ground snapped with incredible violence. In barely three minutes, a rip tore through more than 200 miles of the San Andreas fault. The earth rocked with at least as much force as the 1906 San Francisco quake to the north. As the land shook, livestock tumbled over in fields. Trees whipped in the air as if they were being hit by a typhoon. Just as he rushed outside, the commandant of Fort Tejon, a military outpost near the quake's epicenter 60 miles north of Los Angeles, saw his garrison's buildings collapse around him. Because the region was still lightly settled, apparently only two people were killed.

At its northern end, just before it veers under the sea, the San Andreas fault appears equally locked. Though smaller quakes often occur in the area, most of them are centered on subsidiary faults. From all appearances, the plates have not budged along the big fault since the great disaster that began on the morning of April 18, 1906. Shortly after 5 A.M., while most of the city still slept, a section of rock north of San Francisco's Golden Gate snapped with ferocious might. Blocks on opposite sides of the break lurched past each other by as much as 21 feet. Powerful shocks radiated across a wide swath of California, Nevada, and Oregon. Later geologists found that the rupture extended more than 250 miles along the fault.

The shocks lasted less than two minutes, but in those brief moments of violence, hundreds of small structures built on landfill along the waterfront fell, trapping their occupants inside. Other casualties were San Francisco's newly constructed city hall and several luxury hotels. Thousands of people sought safety in the streets, including some famous visitors. The tenor Enrico Caruso, who was in San Francisco to perform in the opera *Carmen*, wandered about aimlessly in his nightshirt clutching a prized signed photograph of President Theodore Roosevelt. Encountering the actor John Barrymore, still in evening garb from an all-night carouse, the singer mustered a wisecrack: "Mr. Barrymore, you are the only man in the world who would dress for an earthquake." The psychologist William James, who had gone to California specifically to witness a quake, was enraptured. "I felt no trace whatever of fear," he said. "It was pure delight and welcome."

But for most San Franciscans the earthquake was a nightmare.

Fires broke out almost immediately and raged uncontrollably for the next three days because of broken water mains. When looters appeared in the streets, martial law was declared, and soldiers were ordered to shoot transgressors on the spot. There were many poignant scenes. Trapped under an iron girder in the ruins of the St. Katherine Hotel with no hope of getting out, a man begged a passing policeman to shoot him. The officer complied. Another man, desperate to save his two babies after seeing his wife crushed to death, put them into suitcases and fled the smoking city to Oakland across the bay. On his arrival, he found that the tots had suffocated.

When the shaking and burning finally stopped, 2,000 acres of the city—approximately 500 square blocks—had been turned into a wasteland. The downtown business district was destroyed. Barely a trace remained of Chinatown's shanties or of the bawdy Barbary Coast's bars and gambling joints. Food and medical supplies flooded in from all over the country. But even as the last aftershocks vibrated their beloved city, San Franciscans began the job of rebuilding. United by a common tragedy, they vowed to create a new and better San Francisco. Indeed, in their exuberance, they all but ignored the lessons of the earthquake. Although they were confronted everywhere with signs of the seismic nature of the catastrophe—cracked roadways, bent and twisted railroad tracks, breaks in the orderly rows of fruit trees—they preferred to close their eyes to the danger lurking in the ground under them. Building after building went up in highly risky areas, often directly over the fault zone. For years afterward, local boosters spoke, not of a calamitous earthquake, but of The Great San Francisco *Fire* of 1906.

Yet in spite of the ostrichlike behavior of San Franciscans, the threat of future quakes remained as real as the earth itself. The plates were continuing their inexorable movements, pressing by one another as they have been doing since long before the appearance of the first humans on the planet. Rather than ending the seismic dangers confronting San Franciscans, the 1906 quake only gave them a respite, and a brief one at that on any geological time scale. Before long the growing stresses and strains along the San Andreas fault would again bring it to the breaking point. But even the most sophisticated theories and most sensitive instruments cannot say exactly when or where that will happen. The only thing scientists can tell San Franciscans for sure is that one day the earth will again tremble violently.

In 1972 a graduate student at Stanford University named Kerry Sieh decided that if neither seismologists nor their careful measurements could prophesy the San Andreas's future behavior with any precision, perhaps clues might emerge from looking at the fault's past. Sieh realized that scientists had already established a chronology of old quakes from their studies of colonial records, but these documents went back only a few hundred years to the days of the early Spanish settlements. (The Indians kept no written accounts.) A few other quakes in the more distant past had been pinpointed with the help of tree rings (see Chapter 3), but these investigations also had limitations. So Sieh decided to do a little spadework of his own, literally. With axe and shovel, he dug trenches in dried old riverbeds along the San Andreas fault at just those places where they had been offset by past quakes. Here he found what were, in a sense, pages of a seismic history book. The author was nature itself. Each time the fault had fractured in a quake, the break was subsequently silted over by the river flow with a new layer of rock, gravel, and organic material. The ages of these distinct layers, easily identifiable to Sieh from their different colors and consistency, were established by so-called atomic clocks, or radiocarbon techniques. In one peat bog just a few miles northeast of Los Angeles, Sieh found evidence of eight different quakes, ranging as far back as A.D. 565. After examining still other sites, he was able to push the fault's quake history even further back, peeling away layers as old as 6,000 years. On average, he found, big quakes recurred along the San Andreas once every 160 years.

By this reckoning, the next big quake in the area of Los Angeles should come early in the twenty-first century and, if the same pattern holds in the northern part of the state, about 2066 in the San Francisco area. But a major quake was most seriously overdue along the San Andreas's southernmost section, from San Bernardino to the Salton Sea; this leg had not fractured for some 600 years. Sieh was quite properly loathe to tie himself to exact dates. Over the years, his research showed, the San Andreas often ignored the average, shaking as many as 80 years before or after the dates dictated by the statistical timetable. The most Sieh would say was that a great earthquake could hit Southern California in the next decade—or in the next century. His chronology of the San Andreas upheavals supported either conclusion.

Unable to find anything definitive in the seismic past or present, seismologists have lately been turning to the animal world for help. The possibility that lowly beasts might help foretell quakes is not as farfetched as it sounds. For thousands of years, people have looked to living creatures for auguries of the future. The Roman naturalist Pliny wrote that excited birds were a sure sign of the coming of a temblor. The folklore of quake-riddled regions includes many tales of strange animal behavior in the hours before quakes. On May 6, 1976, a magnitude 6.5 quake devastated the Italian alpine region of Friuli, a largely German-speaking area once part of the Austrian Tyrol. Later residents remembered that just before the disaster horses had stirred uneasily in their stables, mice scampered out of basements, deer came down from the hills, and snakes awakened from their midday slumber.

Scientists have been hard pressed to explain the uncanny ability of animals to anticipate quakes, if indeed that is what they are doing. But there are a number of theories. Migratory birds and other animals may be able to foretell tremors by sensing changes in the local magnetic field. Other animals can perhaps hear or feel foreshocks that are too faint to be detected by human senses. After investigating the quake in his hometown in Friuli, a West Berlin chemist named Helmut Tributsch conjectured that the animals' delicate biochemistry may be responding to electrical charges released into the air by the ground's prequake activity.

As evidence, Tributsch cited many historical instances of quakes that were accompanied by an eerie, flickering glow over the ground. He suggested that the phenomenon, known as earthquake lights, could be the product of electrical fields that are created when certain types of crystalline rock like quartz come under high pressure. In fact, a scientist at the University of Arizona, Stuart A. Hoening, reproduced the effect in his laboratory when he stressed rocks to the breaking point and observed flashes around them. Other scientists link earthquake lights to the frictional heat of masses of rock grinding against each other. In the view of some researchers, charged particles in the atmosphere—atomic fragments called ions—may influence human behavior as well by inducing subtle changes in brain chemistry.

Indeed, there is one researcher in the San Francisco area who has organized an informal network of people who claim to be more than normally sensitive to slight physical changes in their environment, like ions in the air. Whenever they feel some physical distress, say, an upset stomach or a headache, they are asked to report their discomfort by telephone at any hour of the day or night. By collecting and analyzing these complaints, Marsha Adams, a biologist and statistician at SRI International (formerly the Stanford Research Institute), says that she has been able to predict six earthquakes. "What she has done," explains a staffer at the U.S. Geological Survey earthquake center in Menlo Park, "is to add the integer of human responsiveness to the other factors in the forecasting equation."

Most seismologists take such assertions with a heavy dose of skepticism, but they are beginning to take more seriously talk of seismic ability in animals. To a large extent, the changing attitude is due to reports out of China, where animal behavior has long been closely observed as a quake precursor. Returning from a trip to China in 1974, Barry Raleigh learned firsthand why the Chinese put such great store in animal reactions. Just before the Hollister quake, he was told, local horses had a bad case of nerves. Many were fidgety, some refused to leave their paddocks. Said Raleigh: "We were skeptical when we arrived in China. But there may be something to [the seismic sensitivity of animals]."

Chinese seismologists certainly think so. They say that just before a quake shook the city of Tientsin in the summer of 1969, animals in the local zoo displayed all sorts of prequake malaise. A Manchurian tiger stopped pacing in its cage. Swans fluttered out of the water. A Tibetan yak collapsed, and an anguished panda buried its head in its paws and moaned. One strong factor that helped persuade Chinese scientists in 1975 that a quake was about to rock Manchuria's Liaoning Province was the number of reports from local communes of extremely weird antics by dogs, cows, horses, and pigs.

In a largely rural country like China, where millions of people live side by side with domestic animals, any abnormality in the way these creatures act is quickly noticed. In fact, the Chinese are openly encouraged from their earliest school years to watch for hints of strange animal behavior, along with other signs of an imminent quake, like changes in the level, color, or taste of well water. To collect such data, China maintains an army of some 10,000 or so amateur seismologists, many of them teenagers. All have been taught to make simple measurements. On a visit to China a few years ago, the author recalls seeing youngsters walking along country roads carrying long, calibrated poles. They used these to check the depth of wells. Even billboards in China advertise the quake danger and remind the public to remain vigilant. In one government pamphlet, peasants are told to be wary when "pigeons are frightened and will not return to their nests, when rabbits with their ears standing jump up or crash into things, when fish jump out of the water as if frightened."

In the urbanized United States, such "barefoot seismology" is not really practical. Most people neither have the experience with animals nor live close enough to nature to tell when something may be amiss in the ground. But American scientists have begun to look for themselves to see whether there is some truth in this folklore about quakes. In hopes of getting an early tip to a possible temblor, University of California scientists placed cages of laboratory mice and rats in the heart of the Palmdale Bulge, watching every twitch of their whiskers for a possible seismic alarm. Other researchers have been testing the keen senses of cockroaches. In Japan, biologists have been trying to find out whether the catfish's legendary talent for causing quakes is matched by one for anticipating them. So far the experiments have produced no definite answers and no simple way to use animals as quake indicators. Fido, it appears, is still no substitute for the seismograph.

If seismologists have learned anything at all from the investigations of quakes, it is that there is no easy solution to the problem of forecasting the earth's rampages. Despite all the theorizing about dilatancy and gaps, despite the putative seismic powers of animals, many quakes seem to strike without any forewarning. In 1979 tremors shook the Coyote Lake region south of San Francisco. Only a short distance from the U.S. Geological Survey's Menlo Park headquarters, the area had been thoroughly rigged with instruments. Scientists had also made provisions for collecting reports on any unexpected animal behavior. Still, the quake took the researchers completely by surprise. They picked up no advance warning whatsoever—no changes in seismic waves, no variations in local magnetism or electrical conductivity of the rock. Later they found that there might have been some effects on well water, but unlike the Chinese they had made no effort to watch for such signs.

And even when scientists think they have spotted some indication of a quake, they may be woefully off the mark. In 1981 two eminent seismologists became convinced that a major quake, perhaps the biggest of the century, would rock Peru that August. The forecast caused a flurry of excitement in scientific circles, to say nothing of the alarm it created in South America. The scientists seemed to have devised a new theory of quake prediction. But August came and went with barely a tremor in the Andean highlands.

The problem confronting would-be predictors is, in a sense, as complex as the earth's crust itself. Even along a single fault like the San Andreas, the shape and structure of the bedrock is so varied from place to place that no two quakes are totally alike. What may constitute warning signs for one section of the fault may be completely irrelevant for another. Yet as seismologists collect more and better information, accumulating data about tremors of every kind, these difficulties should gradually diminish. Predictions will become more and more accurate, perhaps even as good as the daily weather forecasts. Some optimistic seismologists foresee this happening by the end of the century or possibly sooner. But there is one thing scientists may never be able to predict: whether the people who dwell in the area of the likely quake will heed their warnings.

selected bibliography

Bolt, Bruce A. *Earthquakes: A Primer.* San Francisco: W. H. Freeman and Company, 1978.

Calder, Nigel. *The Restless Earth.* New York: Viking Press, 1972.

DeNevi, Don. *Earthquakes.* Millbrae, California: Celestial Arts, 1977.

Eiby, George A. *Earthquakes.* New York: Van Nostrand Reinhold Company, 1980.

Encyclopaedia Britannica, Editors of. *Disaster! When Nature Strikes Back.* Bantam Books, 1978.

Frazier, Kendrick. *The Violent Face of Nature.* New York: William Morrow and Company, 1979.

Gribbin, John. *This Shaking Earth.* New York: G. P. Putnam's Sons, 1978.

Krauskopf, Konrad B. *The Third Planet: An Invitation to Geology.* San Francisco: Freeman, Cooper & Company, 1974.

Ritchie, David. *The Ring of Fire.* New York: Atheneum, 1981.

Scientific American, Readings from. *Continents Adrift and Continents Aground.* San Francisco: W. H. Freeman and Company, 1976.

──────. *Earthquakes and Volcanoes.* San Francisco: W. H. Freeman and Company, 1980.

Shurkin, Joel N. *Update—Report on the Planet Earth*. Philadelphia: Westminster Press, 1976.

Sullivan, Walter. *Continents in Motion*. New York: McGraw Hill, 1974.

Takeuchi, H., Uyeda, S., and Kanamori, H. *Debate about the Earth* (revised edition). San Francisco: Freeman, Cooper & Company, 1970.

Tributsch, Helmut. *When the Snakes Awake: Animals and Earthquake Prediction*. Cambridge: MIT Press, 1982.

Verney, Peter. *The Earthquake Handbook*. New York: Paddington Press, 1979.

Walker, Bryce, and the editors of Time-Life Books. *Earthquake*. Alexandria, Virginia: Time-Life Books, 1982.

Wegener, Alfred. *The Origin of Continents and Oceans* (fourth edition). London: Methuen & Company, 1967.

Wilford, John Noble. *The Mapmakers*. New York: Knopf, 1981.

index

A
Adams, Marsha, 162
Aggarwal, Yash, 140, 149
Algonquins, 20
American Miscellaneous Society, 102, 117
Amundsen, Roald, 77
Anaxagoras, 23
Anderson, Don, xii, xiii, 140
animal behavior, *see* earthquakes, predicting
Aristotle, 23, 30
Arizona, University of, 42
asthenosphere, 121–122
astronauts, ix–x
Atlas, 20
atomic clocks, *see* radioactive dating

B
Babylonians, 21–22, 33
Bache, Alexander Dallas, 108–109
"barefoot seismology," 163
Barrymore, John, 157
Beloussov, Vladimir V., 131
Benioff, Hugo, 116
Bering Sea, 86
Blue Mountain Lake, 140, 149
body waves, 99, *see also* earthquakes, waves
Bolt, Bruce A., 45, 128
Bounty, H.M.S., 130
Brace, William F., 142

C
Caldwell, D. W., xiii
California Institute of Technology, 107
California, University of (Berkeley), 44, 45
Cambridge University, 124
Cape Yakataga, Alaska, 153
Carib Indians, 24–25
Carlsberg Ridge, 124
Caruso, Enrico, 157

catastrophism, 79, 81
Caxton, William, 30
Chang Heng, 37–40, 38 (photograph)
China, 15, 16, 19–20, 37–40
Choko, see Chang Heng
Coimbra, University of, 29
Columbia University, see Lamont-Doherty Geological Observatory
continental drift, 77–78, 81–82, 106, 118, 121–122, 122 (diagram), 132, see also plate tectonics and sea-floor spreading
  applications, 134–135
  as earthquake mechanism, 135
  future, 134
continents
  fit of, 79, 86–87, 90
  structure of, 85–86
convection currents, 119–120
core, 103–105, 119
crust, 102, 114, 119

D

Daly City, Calif., 4, 12
dams, 144–145
Darwin, Charles, 14–15, 80
Darwin, George, 80
Deep Sea Drilling Project, 132
Defense Department, 128
dendrochronology, 40–43, 43 (photograph)
Dietrich, James, 146
Dietz, David S., 121
dilatancy, 142–144, 148, 149

E

earth, ix
  cooling and contracting, 60–61
  formation of, 118–120
  structure of, 102, 103–106, 105 (diagram)
earthquake lights, 161
earthquakes
  Alaska (1964), 11 (photograph), 48, 152
  Ashkhabad, U.S.S.R. (1948), 137
  Assam (1950), 100
  Boston (1755), 8, 31–32
  California (1812), 44
  Charleston, S.C. (1886), 8
  Chile (1835), 14–15; (1960), 14, 48
  controlling, 144–146
  Coyote Lake, Calif. (1979), 164
  damage from, x–xii
  deep-focus, 128
  detecting old, 41–44, 159–160
  explaining, 13–14, 30–35, 53–55, 57–61, 71
  Fort Tejon, Calif. (1857), 156–157
  Friuli, Italy (1976), 160–161
  Haicheng, China (1975), 15–16, 162
  historical view of, x–xi, 18–25, 21 (drawing)
  Hollister, Calif. (1974), 151
  intensity of, 63, see also Modified Mercalli Scale
  Jericho (circa 1100 B.C.), 36

Index

Lisbon (1755), 26–30, 27 (drawing)
London (1750), 25–26
magnitude of, see Richter scale
Manhattan (1893), 9
Massachusetts Bay Colony (1638), 44
measuring, 62–64, 66–68
Naples (1857), 62–64
Neo Valley, Japan (1891), 73
New Madrid, Mo. (1811–1812), 8, 45–46, 48–52
Niigata, Japan (1964), 148
Oaxaca, Mexico (1978), 154–156
predicting, xi, 15–16, 52, 57, 59, 138–139, 141, 146–156, 164–165; with animals, 160–163
risk of, 7–12, 10 (diagram)
Riverside, Calif. (1974), 149–150
San Fernando Valley (1971), 8, 9 (photograph), 140–141
San Francisco (1906), frontispiece, 7, 11, 12, 48, 55, 57, 59, 135, 157–159
San Juan Battista (1800), 44
San Juan Capistrano (1812), 44
sea-floor, 112–113, 115–116
shallow, 128
Shensi, China (1556), 37
Sitka, Alaska (1979), 153
Tangshan, China (1976), 16
Tashkent, U.S.S.R. (1966), 147
Tientsin, China (1969), 162
Tokyo (1855), 18
waves of, 34, 38, 39, 49, 54–55, 65, 71–72, 97–103; changing velocities of, 138–144, 151–152
Zagreb (1909), 96–97, 101–102, 103
East Pacific Rise, 126
elastic rebound theory, 57, 58 (diagram), 59
epicenter, 64, 72, 72 (diagram)
Eskimos, see Inuits
Evans, David M., 144
Ewing, James Alfred, 70
Ewing, Maurice, 109–111, 110 (photograph), 112–113, 131

F

faults, 50, 55, 71
 strike-slip, 150
 thrust, 150
Fedotov, S.A., 152
Feyzóo y Montenegro, Benito Jéronimo, 33
focus, 64
Forel, F.A., 100
Franciscans, 44
Franklin, Benjamin, 31, 108–109

G

gaps, seismic, 152–156
Garm District, 136–138
Garmany, John, 140
Genesis, Book of, 79
geophones, 49
Glomar Challenger, 132–133
Glossopteris, 80–81
Gomorrah, 36

Gondwanaland, 81, 85
gravity, 61, 84, 114
Gray, Thomas, 70
Great Neopolitan Earthquake of 1867, 65
Greeks, 22–24
Greenland, 75, 77, 78, 83, 91, 92–95
Gutenberg, Beno, 103–107
Gutenberg Discontinuity, 105
Guyot, Arnold H., 114
guyots, 114–115

H
Halley's comet, 16
Healy, John, 151
Heezen, Bruce, 108, 112–113
Helmont, J. B. von, 25
Herculaneum, 24
Hess, Harry H., 114–115, 117–123
Hoening, Stuart A., 161
Hollister, Calif., 44, 150–151
Holmes, Arthur, 94, 120, 121
Humboldt, Alexander von, 79
Hutton, James, 81

I
ice ages, 86
International Geophysical Year, 113
Inuits, 75, 75 (footnote)
isoseismals, 64
isostasy, 85
Ivo, Miguel Tibero Pedegache Brandão, 33

J
Jacob, Klaus, 153
James, William, 157
Japan, 18–19, 37, 68, 73, 139, 147–148
Jeffreys, Harold, 91
Johnston, Malcolm, 151
Jupiter Effect, 22 (footnote)
Justinian, 25

K
Kamchatka Peninsula, 21, 146, 152
Kashima, 18–19
Khait, 136
Köppen, Else, 87
Köppen, Peter, 87
Koto, Bunjiro, 71

L
Lamont-Doherty Geological Observatory, 108
land bridges, 85–86
Latham, Gary, 154
Lilienthal, Theodor Christoph, 79
lithosphere, 121, 130
Los Angeles, 8, 17
Louderback, George, 44, 45
Love, A. E. H., 100
Love waves, 100–101
Lowell, Percival, 131
Lucretius, 24
Lyell, Charles, 81

Index

M
Magellan, Ferdinand, 108
magma, 54
magnetism, terrestrial, 113–114, 123–125
magnetometers, 113
Mallet, Robert, 62–65, 128, 143
mantle, 102, 104–105, 119, 120, 121
Marianas trench, 114
Mars, "canals" of, 131
Massachusetts Institute of Technology, 142
Matthews, Drummond H., 124
Matumoto, Tosimatu, 154
McCann, William, 153
McNally, Karen, 154–156, 155 (photograph)
Mercalli, Giuseppi, see Modified Mercalli Scale
Mesosaurus, 84–86
Meteor, 112
Michell, John, 34–35
microseisms, 3
Mid-Atlantic Ridge, 112, 113, 124
Mid-Ocean Ridge, 112, 121, 127 (diagram)
Milne, John, 68–74
Mirrour of the World, 30
Mississippi River, 46
Modified Mercalli Scale, 63 (footnote)
Mogi, Kiyo, 153
Mohole, Project, 102, 117
Mohorovičić, Andrija, 96–97, 101–103
Mohorovičić Discontinuity (Moho), 102
Mongolians, 20
Montana, 128
Morley, Lawrence W., 125
Moses, 36
mountains, building of, 60, 90
Mount Sinai, 36

N
namazu, 18
Nature, 125
Neptune, see Poseidon
Newton, Isaac, 33–34, 60, 84
Noah's flood, 79
nuclear explosions, detecting, 128, 129
Nur, Amos, 142

O
Oakland, Calif., 4
ocean floor, exploration of, 107–116
Old Testament, 36
Oldham, Richard D., 103
Ohtake, Masakazu, 154
Origin of Continents and Oceans, The, 87–88

P
P waves, 97–99, 98 (diagram), 109, see also earthquake waves, changing velocities
Palmdale Bulge, 148–149, 163
Pangaea, 88, 89 (diagram), 94, 133

Panthalassa, 88
Perez, Omar, 153
Pericles, 23
Perry, Matthew, 69
Persians, 20
Peru, 164
Philosophy of Earthquakes, 31
Pignataro, Domenico, 63
Placet, François, 79
plate tectonics, 61, 122–123, 133–134
Pliny, the Elder, 24, 36–37, 160
Pompeii, 24
Poseidon, 22
Princeton University, 114, 115, 117
Pythagoras, 23–24

Q
quakes, *see* earthquakes

R
radioactive dating, 125
radioactivity, 60–61
Raleigh, C. Barry, xiii, 145–146, 162
Rangely oil field, 145
Rayleigh, Lord, 100
Rayleigh waves, 100, 101, *see also* earthquakes, waves
Reid, Harry Fielding, 55, 57–59
Reynolds, Osborne, 141–142
Richter, Charles F., 46, 47 (photograph), 107
Richter scale, 46–48, 107
rift valleys, 112
Ring of Fire, 65, 128, 153

Rocky Mountain Arsenal, 144
Romans, 24
Rousseau, Jean-Jacques, 30

S
S waves, 97–99, 98 (diagram), *see also* earthquake waves, changing velocities
Saint Lawrence River Valley, 8
Saint Louis University, 50–51
San Andreas fault, 4, 7, 13, 15, 42, 44, 48, 56 (photograph), 135, 156–157, 159–160, 164
San Francisco, 1–7, 10–13, *see also* earthquakes
scarps, 40
Scholz, Christopher, xiii, 142, 143 (photograph)
Scott, Robert Falcon, 77
sea-floor sediment, 111
sea-floor spreading, 121, 129
rates of, 126, 132–133
seamounts, *see* guyots
seiche, 100
seismic profiling, 49
seismogram, 68, 97, 98 (diagram)
seismograph, 38–40, 67 (diagram), 68, 70–71, 97
seismology, xi, 65
seismometer, 66–67
seismoscope, 40, 66
shadow zone, 103–104, 104 (diagram)
Sherlock, Thomas, 26
Shide Circulars, 74
Sieh, Kerry, 159–160
Snider-Pellegrini, Antonio, 79–80

Index

Sodom, 36
South Pole, 77
Soviet Union, earthquake activities, 136–140
SRI International, 162
Stevenson, Adlai, ix
Strabo, 23
strata, 49
Stukeley, William, 31
subduction, 116
Suess, Eduard, 33, 80–81, 85
Sumatra, 20, 154
surface waves, 99–101, *see also* earthquakes, waves
Surtsey, 112
Sykes, Lynn R., xiii, 129–130, 139, 149, 153

T

Texas (Galveston), University of, 154
Tonga trench, 115, 130
transform faults, 126–127, 127 (diagram), 129
Tributsch, Helmut, 161
tsunamis, 23

U

uniformitarianism, 81
United Nations, ix

Urey, Harold, 119
U.S. Geological Survey, 42, 49, 50, 125, 150

V

Velikovsky, Immanuel, 117–118
Vema, 109–110
Vening Meinesz, Felix Andries, 114
Venus, 118
Verne, Jules, 105
Vesuvius, Mount, 24
Vine, Frederick J., 123–126
Voltaire, 30

W

Wadata, Kiyoo, 116
Wegener, Alfred Lothar, 75–95, 76 (photograph)
Wesley, John, 25
Whitcomb, James, 140, 149
Wiechert, Emil, 103
Wight, Isle of, 73
Wilson, J. Tuzo, 125–127, 130, 131
Winthrop, John IV, 32, 34
Worlds in Collision, 117

Y

Yugoslavia, 96

A000009576810

WITHDRAWN